a man's

place is behind

tucker shaw

the bar

PHOTOGRAPHS
BY LEIGH BEISCH

killer cocktail recipes

SAN FRANCISCO CHRONICLE BOOKS

Library of Congress Cataloging-in-Publication Data available.

ISBN 978-0-8118-5577-8

Manufactured in China.

Designed *by* Jay Peter Salvas while tanked.
Food and prop styling *by* George Dolese.
This book was typeset in Helvetica Neue 8/13.
The photographer wishes to thank her assistant
   Lauren Grant and her studio manager Shana Lopes,
   as well as Chronicle Books, Jay Peter Salvas, and
   Tucker Shaw for letting her in on the fun.
The prop stylist wishes to thank Elisabet Der Nederlanden
   and Elise Ravet for their lovely food styling assistance.

10 9 8 7 6 5 4 3 2 1

Chronicle Books LLC
680 Second Street
San Francisco, California 94107

www.chroniclebooks.com

dedication

This book is for Ray Rinaldi, Daniel Tseng, and Andy Fishering. Cheers, boys.

acknowledgments

Continued thanks to Dan Mandel.

Thanks to Bill LeBlond: Where would I be without you?

To Amy Treadwell, where would Bill or I be without you?

To Mikyla Bruder, forever and always.

To Jennifer Tomaro, Carrie Bradley, Doug Ogan, Evan Hulka, Jennifer Sparkman, Peter Perez, and everyone at Chronicle Books, the coolest house ever.

To Jay P. Salvas, killer designer and big-hearted man: You conceived this project in the first place. Thanks, big J.

Thanks to Jenn, Michael, Elliott James, and Auntie Banana.

Thanks to Chris and Doc.

Thanks to the Shady Pines crew, you bunch of shameless lushes.

Thanks to Eric, who prefers wine but has been known to suck down a martini in a pinch. To Mom, for keeping an eye on Momofuku for me.

Thanks to my excellent nephew Will, who asked me to mention him in this book though it seems inappropriate since he's well underage but what the hell.

Eternal thanks to Leigh Beisch, George Dolese, and their most awesome studio crew.

table of

content

A good cocktail, carefully balanced and lovingly mixed, is one of life's greatest pleasures.

Sure, there are purists out there who bemoan mixed drinks as nonsense, gussied-up concoctions meant for people who can't handle unadorned alcohol.

And they have a point. Many dollars are spent and made on sugary beverages meant to get you drunker faster, which, while it makes for riveting reality TV, is no good for your body or soul, and unfair to spirits manufacturers, who labor with great energy and passion to create their nectars.

But the truth is, well-mixed cocktails don't disguise the spirits within. Just the opposite: A hit of vermouth opens up gin's hidden botanic qualities.

A drop or two of bitters brings rum to attention. And neat bourbon, while noble, is no match for a mint julep on race day.

The key to mixing good cocktails is restraint. Pour lightly and mix with attention and care. Less is often more. Your goal isn't to get wasted, it's to enjoy the flavors of your drink and toast the end of the day. And if you get a little buzz on, that's just gravy.

A man who mixes a good drink is a better man. Mix yourself a drink.

And now, a few words about responsible drinking.

Don't be a jackass. Call a cab.

Enough said.

Molecular
   Weight : 46.0=

MELting
   Point :

-1

Ethanol
$$C_2H_6O$$

Booze 101: A Diluted Primer on Your Building Blocks

Now that you've probably already made a few drinks in this book without bothering to read this section, take a few moments now to school yourself, however briefly, on the chemistry you're recklessly toying with.

Ethanol is a natural chemical, produced by fermentation. When you take something containing natural sugar *(like berries, grape juice, or yak milk)* and add the right kind of yeast, then deny it access to oxygen *(like in a barrel, bottle, or a tightly closed yak stomach)*, the yeast eats the sugar and produces ethanol, which is the stuff that gets you drunk.

Here's the equation: Juice + yeast - oxygen + time = Let's party.

Humans have been imbibing since prehistory, fermenting anything we could get our hands on: grapes, honey, rice, milk, potatoes.

So when we tinker with cocktails, we're drawing on thousands of years of experimentation. Here is a guide to your arsenal.

gin

Robust and pungent and unmistakably alcoholic, gin
is full of muscle. Its piercing flavor means gin is
rarely drunk neat, except by very heavy gin drinkers[*]
with honorary barstools in one or more local taverns.
Instead, gin is the preferred spirit behind some of the
most iconic cocktails we have, including the undis-
puted emperor of cocktails, the classic martini *(see
page 54)*.

(see page 54).

Gin is made by mixing a neutral spirit *(flavorless
fermented grain, usually corn or barley but sometimes
wheat, rye, or sugarcane)* with botanic-based flavors
*(always juniper berries, but also lemon, orange, anise,
coriander, and other stuff)*, then distilling the mixture
to remove impurities and excess water. Some manufacturers further flavor their gin with botanical essences.

Gin's character comes from its high alcohol content
(usually around 100 proof, or 50 percent alcohol) and
the stuff that's added to it. Gins from different manufacturers can be very different from one another, so buy
a few small bottles and identify your favorite. Then, buy
a gallon.

*Heavy gin drinkers can
also be identified by swollen
red noses.

vodka

Vodka, like all booze, is a product of fermenting and
distilling and filtering stuff. In the case of vodka, the
stuff could be almost anything: potatoes or corn or
wheat or rice, or even grapes or sugar. Most vodkas
are around 80–100 proof, or 40–50 percent alcohol.

The purest vodkas are exhaustively distilled and filtered
to get rid of any flavor or texture left over from whatever was fermented in the first place. Because it has so
little flavor, vodka's a perfect mixing spirit, a clean slate.

Some vodkas have added flavors like orange or lemon or coffee or pepper. While this might seem like a needless bastardization of a perfectly good product,[*] the truth is, people have been flavoring vodka for centuries.

*See also: flavored colas, "Cool Ranch" anything.

whiskey

Whiskey is the Big Daddy of booze. Its roster of offspring includes bourbon, Scotch, Irish whiskey, and rye, each of which takes the basic whiskey-making process *(fermenting a mix of mashed-up grains, or mash, distilling the liquid, then aging it in oak barrels)* in a slightly different direction.

Bourbon comes from in and around Bourbon County, Kentucky. It's made from a mash that's mostly corn, then aged for at least 2 years in oak barrels that have been charred on the inside, which adds color and depth to the whiskey.

*The Scottish (and Canadians) lose the "e" and spell it "whisky." Efficient bastards.

Scotch whisky[*] is made from germinated, or *malted*, barley that's been dried over a fire before it's fermented, so it tastes slightly smoky. It's aged in oak barrels for at least 3 years.

Irish whiskey, like Scotch, is made from grain, usually malted and usually barley, but the mash isn't dried before fermenting, so theret's no smokiness.

Rye whiskey, which includes some Canadian whiskies and many American ones, is made from a mash that's mostly, if not all, rye, which makes it sort of spicy.

Blended whiskies are made using different grains in varying proportions, mixed and matched to produce a specific end result: smoothness, spiciness, woodsiness, etc.

rum

It's no accident that rum is the sweetest spirit in the cupboard—it's made from sugarcane.

Sugarcane juice or molasses *(the gooey stuff left over after sugarcane is processed into sugar)* is fermented and distilled, then aged in barrels *(either wood or steel)* to develop color and flavor.

It's also no accident that rum is the basis for tropical drinks like daiquiris and mojitos—most of it is made in the Caribbean.*

*This is also why it is popular with pirates.

Rums come in a whole range of colors, depending on how long they've been aged and how aggressively they've been filtered before bottling. Light rums and white rums are thoroughly filtered and aged only for a short time. Dark rums are filtered less and aged longer. Lighter rums are usually better for mixing, while darker rums are sometimes best poured over a few rocks and sipped neat.

tequila

Tequila is actually a subset of mescal, a family of alcohols made from the blue agave plant, which grows in Mexico and looks kind of like an aloe vera plant. Tequila is made in the western Mexican region of, believe it, Tequila. The agave* is chopped up, cooked, mashed, fermented in pots, distilled, and aged in oak barrels.

*Good tequilas are 100 percent agave. "Mixto" tequilas often add cane sugar to the mix.

The amount of aging determines the type of tequila. *Plata* or *blanco*, or silver, tequilas are bottled soon after distilling. *Oro*, or gold, tequilas often spend some time in barrels, plus get a shot of caramel for color. *Reposado* hangs in the barrels for 2–12 months. *Añejo*, the grand-daddy of tequila, ages for at least a year, if not several.

In general, the younger the tequila, the better it is for mixing. Old tequilas deserve to be sipped neat.

brandy

Brandy, like wine, is made from fruit, usually grapes. In fact, before brandy is brandy it is wine, but then it's distilled again* and aged. It can also be made from apples *(Calvados)*, pears *(poire)*, peaches, plums—pretty much whatever's growing on that tree out back.

*Making it twice as alcoholic as wine.

There are several types of brandy. Cognac is always made in the Cognac region of France. It's distilled, twice, from grapes in a copper still, then aged in oak barrels for several years. While it ages, it's blended with younger and older batches to achieve the producer's signature balance, and to maintain the same flavor every year.

Armagnac is made farther south in France. It's also made from grapes, but distilled only once, then aged in darker wood for a longer time. It's also not usually blended, so each year's batch is slightly different from the year before.

The best brandies are for sipping, always. But everyday brandies are great for mixing.

liqueur

Liqueur, which is a word you have to say with pursed lips to get it to sound right, is made by infusing alcohol with things like herbs, fruit, coffee, or whatever. Schnapps, Midori, Kahlúa, Cointreau, crème de menthe, Baileys . . . all of these are liqueurs. You can drink most liqueurs straight-up, but they're usually incredibly sweet. They are much more useful in mixed drinks, where they'll add a punch of flavor, and often color, without adding a whole lot of extra booze to your already irresponsibly alcoholic cocktail.*

The most-used liqueurs in my cabinet are Cointreau *(for margaritas)* and Campari *(for negronis)*.

*Most liqueurs are about 30–60 proof, or about 15–30 percent alcohol.

beer

Beer is—well, if you don't know what beer is, check the fridge. It's a fermented and filtered, but not distilled, brew of hops, barley, and water. It's best consumed cold,* and by itself, but in some cases makes an excellent mixer.

*I don't care what the English say, beer is better when it's cold.

wine

Wine is the fermented juice of fruit, almost always grapes. It's also not distilled. The best wines are naturally best drunk on their own, but some everyday wines make great mixers for sangria and other stuff.

Champagne and other bubbly wines (like Italian *prosecco*, Spanish *cava*, or other sparklers) are refermented to produce and trap carbon dioxide, i.e., bubbles. Their effervescence makes excellent textural mixers.

Vermouth is wine that's been jacked up with aromatic herbs and spices. There are two kinds: sweet and dry. Sweet vermouth is best sipped on its own or with a twist. Dry vermouth, with its thick texture and bitter taste, is better as a mixer, the perfect foil to gin in a martini.

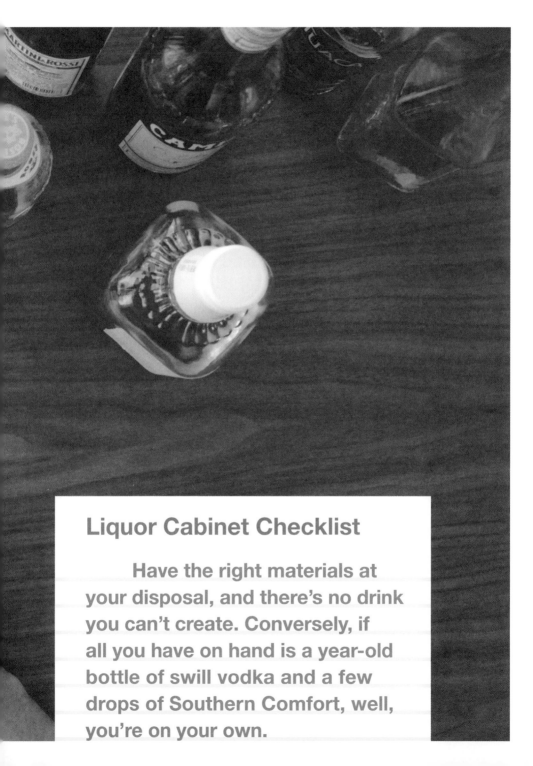

Liquor Cabinet Checklist

Have the right materials at your disposal, and there's no drink you can't create. Conversely, if all you have on hand is a year-old bottle of swill vodka and a few drops of Southern Comfort, well, you're on your own.

The first step in smart drinks mixing is smart purchasing. Check your liquor supply once a month to make sure you have staples on hand. Last thing you need is an empty gin bottle when you need a martini most.

If you find any bottle less than one-quarter full, make a round of drinks with it and add it to your shopping list. If there are bottles in there that you've had for more than a few months, toss them. *(Long-term exposure to oxygen renders booze sour and unpalatable.)*

If you're planning a big blowout, stock up on extra stuff, and always plan for 30 percent more than you think you need.

If you don't yet have liquor-brand loyalties, do this: Buy small bottles of several different brands and conduct a taste test. Besides being fun, it's the only way you'll be able to tell Tanqueray from Hendrick's from Beefeater.

Like with shoes, you don't need to buy the most expensive stuff on the shelf, but you should buy the best you can afford. If your ingredients suck, so will your drinks. Aim high.

requireds

1 bottle premium gin for martinis and negronis et al.

1 bottle second-rate gin for rickeys and slushes et al.

1 bottle premium vodka for martinis and sipping

1 bottle second-rate vodka for mixing

1 bottle dark rum

1 bottle light rum

1 bottle white tequila for mixing

1 bottle *reposado* or *añejo* tequila for shots or sipping

1 bottle mixing brandy

1 bottle sipping Cognac *(ask for this on your birthday)*

1 bottle Scotch whisky

1 bottle bourbon whiskey

1 bottle Irish whiskey

1 bottle Canadian or rye whisky

1 small bottle dry vermouth
for martinis

1 small bottle sweet vermouth
for negronis

1 bottle triple sec and/or
Cointreau

1 bottle Campari

optionals

Kahlúa

Benedictine

Jägermeister

Amaretto

Applejack

Crème de menthe

Drambuie

no kidding

At least 12 beers in the fridge

At least 6 bottles wine *(3 bottles each of red and white)*,
some cheap (but good) for everyday drinking, some
pricey for nights that matter. Chat with the salesperson
at the wine shop who can't wait to help you.

At least 2 bottles champagne, *prosecco*, *cava*, or other
sparkling wine. Make them both good, but make one
extra good. Use the not-extra-good bottle for mixing.

TICKET

12

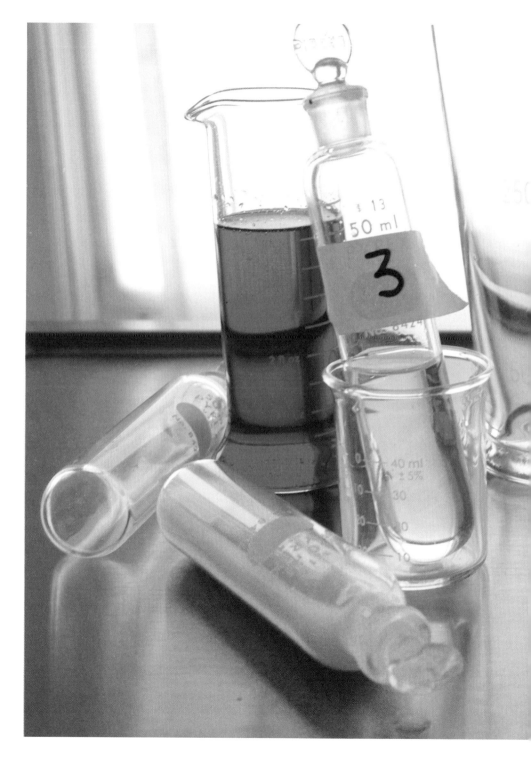

Mixers

Contrary to what you were led to believe in your underage drinking years, mixers are not meant to disguise the alcohol they accompany. Your mixers—tonics, sodas, juices—are meant to frame, enhance, season, and elevate the qualities of the booze in your drink.

Mixers are not afterthoughts, and their purchase and care requires attention.

After all, you could have the nicest bottle of tequila on the planet, but as soon as you add junky store-bought sour mix to it, you might as well be sucking straight from the bottom shelf. First-rate drinks require first-rate mixers.

diluters

fruit juices *(lemon, lime, orange, grapefruit, pineapple, tomato, cranberry, etc.)*

I usually juice my own limes and lemons, and there's no substitute for fresh-squeezed orange or grapefruit juice. Watermelon juice is ridiculously easy to make —just throw some chunks in the blender, let it rip, and strain it through a fine-mesh sieve. But most juices *(apple, tomato, cranberry)* I just buy. Get the freshest you can find.

ice

Ice is only as good as the water it's made from. Not to suggest you should make your cubes from a $4 bottle, but filter it if you can. If you have an ice dispenser in your fridge, change the filter twice a year. Cubes *("rocks")* for serving or stirring drinks should be large. Never shake or stir a drink with crushed ice, as it will dilute too quickly. Save the crushed ice for blender drinks.

water

If the water out of your tap tastes like metal, use water from a bottle. And always add less than you think you'll need, adjusting up if necessary.

fizzers

club soda *(seltzer)* and sparkling water

The best way to add fizz to a drink without adding flavor. Keep it cold so when you add it to your drink it won't melt the ice. Be sure to taste club soda or sparkling water before you add it—some brands have a slightly metallic taste. Also consider bubble size—

smaller bubbles give a subtler fizz, bigger bubbles are brassier. Buy small containers of several brands at first, then choose a favorite and stock up.

sodas

Keep these *(cola, 7UP, ginger ale, etc.)* cold, or else when you add them to your cold cocktail they'll melt your ice too fast and dilute the whole effect. I usually avoid diet sodas as mixers, as they can give that weird artificial-sweetener taste to the cocktail.

tonic

Another fizzy addition, but this one has a slightly bitter flavor to counteract herbal or botanical qualities of some alcohols, specifically gin. The flavor comes from quinine, a powder harvested from a tropical tree in South America, which also prevents malaria. So drink up.

flavorers

bitters

Bitters, which belong in drinks like slings and screw-drivers, are intensely flavored alcohol infusions made with fruits and bitter-flavored herbs that no one's ever heard of *(like gentian and quassia)*. Drunk alone, they are, well, bitter. But in a mix, they add an addictive, slightly astringent flavor note. There are several on the market with different recipes and derivatives, but Angostura and Peychaud's bitters are the most common and most useful. Use sparingly. *(Although people sometimes encourage each other to do shots of these, they're much, much better when mixed into a drink.)*

grenadine

Gives a little sweetness to whatever it's added to, but more importantly, gives a bright burst of red or pink color, depending on how diluted it is. Good to have on hand in case the twelve-and-under set come over for drinks—make Shirley Temples with a marinated cherry or two, a splash of grenadine, ice, and ginger ale.

hot sauce and worcestershire sauce

Bloody Mary's require a few hits of hot sauce *(like Tabasco or Tapatío)* and Worcestershire sauce, which is a fermented blend of vinegar, sugar, chiles, anchovies, and aromatics like garlic and onions. For both hot sauces and Worcestershire sauces, the key is, use as much as you like, and no more. Go light at first, adding more if you need it.

rose's lime juice

This syrupy stuff is never a substitute for fresh lime juice, but sometimes makes a tart addition to sweet drinks.

sweeteners

simple syrup

Simple syrup, is, simply, sugar dissolved in water. You need it for drinks that require sugar *(rickeys, daiquiris)* so you don't get a bunch of undissolved sugar crystals at the bottom of your glass. It's ridiculously easy to make *(see facing page)*.

sour mix

Sour mix is simple syrup flavored *(intensely)* with lemon juice, and buffered for strength with a beaten egg white. *(Don't worry, it doesn't taste like egg.)*

It adds a sour flavor to your drink, as well as a solid froth, and is irreplaceable in margaritas and whiskey sours. Most store-bought mixes suck, so make your own *(see below)*.

Simple Syrup *(makes 1 cup)*

If you want to jack up your syrup, you can steep things like vanilla beans, fresh ginger, cloves, or mint leaves that you've bashed with the back of a spoon in it while it cools. Just remember to strain them out before you store the syrup.

2   cups **sugar**

1   cup **water**

Stir the sugar and water together in a saucepan and heat until it boils. Reduce the heat and simmer, stirring often, for about 5 minutes. Let cool. Done. You can refrigerate it, in a bottle with a tight cap, for up to 2 months.

Sour Mix *(makes about 1 cup)*

Juice of 4 **lemons** *(about ½ cup)*

½ cup **simple syrup**, cooled *(see above)*

1   small **egg white**, beaten

Toss everything into a jar and shake vigorously. Done. Use immediately, or keep it in the fridge for up to 2 weeks.

Garnishes

Unlike a sprig of parsley next to a tuna steak, a garnish is truly an integral and necessary component of a good cocktail. In all cases, they add flavor and good visuals to your drink. A Gibson just isn't a Gibson without a cocktail onion, a mojito nothing without its mint. Do your drinks right and garnish with care.

cherries

Marinated cherries *(usually called maraschino cherries; long story, look it up)* are sweet, richly colored cherries that have been colored and stewed in syrup. The red ones have a faint almond flavor, and the green ones are sort of minty.

Use sweet, syrupy cherries in sweeter, darker drinks like Tom Collinses or Manhattans. After you open the jar, use your cherries within a month or two, and don't be afraid to double them up in tall drinks.

citrus

No trip to the grocery store is complete without the purchase of several limes, lemons, and oranges, just in case. They'll last a couple of weeks. Citrus garnishes belong in all kinds of drinks, from crisp martinis to tropical rum drinks.

There are several ways to cut and use citrus.

round

A round is a circular slice from the center, or equator, of the fruit. If you have seeds in your rounds, poke 'em out with the tip of your knife, or you'll be drinking them. Rounds are great for lining the bottom of your glass, or floating in the middle of your drink.

wedge

A wedge is half of a thick round that's been split into half-circles, usually perched on the rim of the glass or floated on top of the drink. If you want more flavor in your drink *(if you like your gin and tonics limey, for instance)*, use a bigger wedge, or slice your citrus lengthwise instead of across the equator. Squeeze it over your drink just before cheers.

twist

A twist is a small shaving of the citrus peel. Citrus fruits carry most of their juice inside, but most of their flavor in the rind. When making a twist, draw your zester carefully along an unblemished face of the fruit, being careful to minimize the amount of pith you pick up. And do it over the drink, so the oils that spritz off it land in the glass. With practice and experimentation, you'll learn how to create twist variations, like long spirals, short stubbies, and if you're really good, intricate Chinese characters.

cucumber

Sound strange? Try it anyway. The clean, fresh, barely bitter flavor of cucumber makes an excellent alternative to a twist in a vodka martini.

mint

Irreplaceable in juleps and mojitos, mint can be a really annoying garnish if not used correctly. The right way to deal with mint is to muddle, or bruise, the leaves so that they release their oils. Let the leaves stay whole. If you chop them, they'll get stuck in your teeth, and the benefits of serving a mojito to your date will be negated.

You can also incorporate mint in a simple syrup *(see page 29)*.

olives

A green olive is the classic martini garnish. Some come stuffed with pimiento peppers, some stuffed with blue cheese, some stuffed with anchovy. Experiment, and play around with different brands and types of olives. If you ask me, the straight green olive is best—big, briney, and beautiful.

For a martini, just toss a couple olives into the bottom of your glass before pouring. To get a little fancier, skewer three of the little babies on a toothpick or cocktail skewer.

For a dirty martini, add a little splash of the juice from the olive jar to the bottom of the glass. Your cocktail will have more body and flavor.

Keep olives fresh. If your opened jar of olives is a month old, have a martini party to get rid of them, then replace with a new jar.

onions

Garnish your martini with marinated cocktail onions, and your drink is now a Gibson. Treat these the same as you would olives—either toss 'em in the bottom of your cocktail glass, or skewer them in groups of three.

If you like the flavor, add a splash of the marinating juice to the bottom of your glass.

Keep these guys fresh. Use them within a month or so.

salt and sugar

The classic garnish for margaritas, salt is used sparingly, and on the rim of the glass, rather than in the drink itself. Always keep salt on the *outside* rim of the glass, never inside. You don't want it dissolving into your drink. Just a light coating of salt crystals is plenty.

Usually sugar acts as an ingredient in a drink, shaken or stirred into the mix or suspended into syrup to add sweetness. Other times it's used as a rim, using the same technique as with salt. Sugar cubes are also often dropped into Champagne cocktails to encourage more bubbles.

To rim a glass, make a bed of salt or sugar in a small plate or shallow bowl. Lightly moisten the outer rim of the glass by rubbing it with a wedge of lime, then carefully roll the outside of the rim in the bed of salt or sugar.

other stuff

Grated nutmeg and cinnamon are important additions to hot toddies, hot apple ciders, eggnogs, and the like. Some sweet-hot peppers *(like the peppadew)* work great in vodka martinis; some people like bay leaves in their gin martinis. Blackberries and raspberries work in Champagne cocktails. Some people like celery in their Bloody Marys.

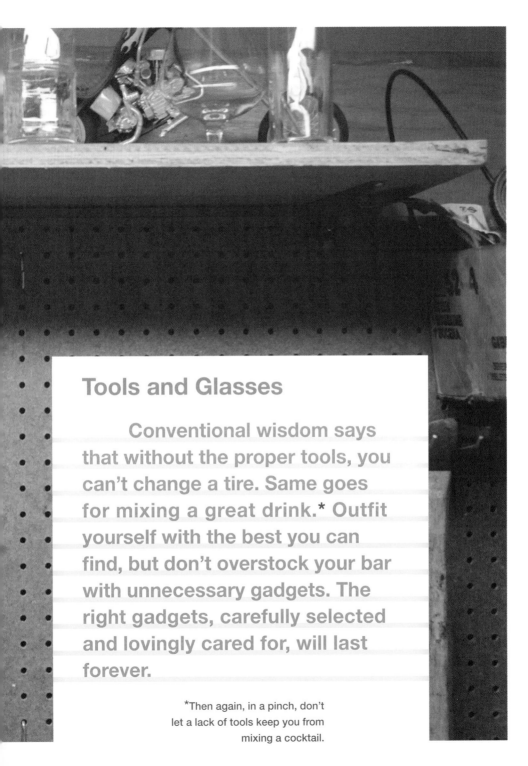

Tools and Glasses

Conventional wisdom says that without the proper tools, you can't change a tire. Same goes for mixing a great drink.* Outfit yourself with the best you can find, but don't overstock your bar with unnecessary gadgets. The right gadgets, carefully selected and lovingly cared for, will last forever.

*Then again, in a pinch, don't let a lack of tools keep you from mixing a cocktail.

tools

bar glass

A stand-alone utility glass, or half of a Boston shaker setup *(see facing page)*. Thick-walled glass goblet used primarily for mixing, not drinking.* Typically 16 ounces, with measurements marked on the side of the glass.

*Although if you slug straight from your bar glass, more power to you.

blender

Do yourself a favor and spend a little extra cash on a good-quality, solid countertop blender. Don't bother with the cheapo version that's on sale; it'll get tired and collapse after a few months of heavy use. You don't need 10 or 15 settings; just on and off will do. Look for a bar blender rather than a kitchen blender, and be sure you can stick all the moving parts in the dishwasher, or you'll lose your mind trying to clean it.

church key and corkscrew

As history progresses, the corkscrew will likely become obsolete, as the truth is there's no reason why wine can't be bottled and kept just as well with a screw-top. But until then, get a good basic corkscrew, sometimes called a "waiter's friend." As to a church key, there's no reason to open your beer bottle with your teeth.

citrus reamer

Don't ever, *ever*, let me catch you with one of those plastic lemons filled with so-called lemon juice. That stuff ain't right. Lemons and limes are ridiculously easy to extract juice from. Simply cut them in half, then ream out with a wooden reamer. Catch the seeds in your hand, or in a small sieve.

cocktail shakers—cobbler and boston

There are two main types of cocktail shakers, the cobbler and the Boston. The cobbler shaker is the most common cocktail shaker. It's normally made of three metal pieces: a large tumbler; a lid with a wide end that fits snugly over the mouth of the tumbler and tapers to a pour spout with a built-in strainer; and a small cap that fits over the pour spout. It's a no-brainer to use. You simply fill it, cap it, shake, then strain into your glass. *(See Chapter 6 for more specifics on shaking.)*

The Boston really isn't a shaker at all but is a large metal tumbler *(about 28 ounces)* and a somewhat smaller glass tumbler *(about 16 ounces, also referred to as a bar glass; see facing page)* with measuring lines on it. It's more versatile but also more difficult to master. The two pieces are inverted into each other mouth-to-mouth for shaking, or used separately for more gentle stirring or pouring. You need a standard handheld bar strainer *(see page 40)* to use with a Boston. For tips on how to shake, stir, or pour drinks, see Chapter 6.

ice bucket

The fastest way to chill down a bottle of wine isn't to put it in the freezer. You'll just forget it's there and it'll eventually explode or something. Instead, fill an ice bucket halfway with ice water and submerge your bottle. Wait 15 minutes. Perfect.

measuring shot glass

Mixing drinks can be a loosey-goosey affair, and there's no reason you can't just eyeball your highball, rather than measuring exactly 2 ounces of booze and 6 of mixer. But some drinks, like a negroni or a stinger, require fairly precise quantities to get the right balance. So get over it and measure. *(Quick glossary: Jigger = 1½ ounces. Pony = 1 ounce. Shot = however much you feel like pouring.)*

muddler

Another item you don't really *need*, but which is great to have: basically a blunt-ended stick used to do things like bruise mint at the bottom of your glass before pouring your mojito. Muddlers are cheap, too. If you don't have one, you can fake it with the handle of a wooden spoon.

paring knife

How else are you going to slice those limes? Buy a high-quality paring knife *(expect to spend around $40–50)* and keep it sharp, and it will last forever. Don't ever put it in the dishwasher.

pitcher

What's better than a shaker full of martini? A pitcher. If you're mixing 4 or more cocktails, use a pitcher so you can pour them all at once. Garnish each glass individually.

stirrer

A long spoon. You don't need one made specifically for cocktails, but they're cheap, so what the hell.

strainers—hawthorn and julep

There are two kinds of strainers: Hawthorn *(a metal disc with a long handle and hole punctures on one side, plus a metal coil underneath to help secure it in the mouth of the shaker or bar glass)* and julep *(an oval-shaped spoon with holes in it)*. They say you should use the Hawthorn when pouring shaken drinks, and the julep when pouring stirred drinks from the bar glass, but I've lived most of my life with just a Hawthorn and it works just fine, thanks. Simply cap the bar glass or shaker with the strainer, hold it down with your thumb, and pour the liquid out the edge of the strainer or through the holes, whatever the size of your glass calls for.

zester

If you're really handy with your knife, you don't need a zester. But if you'd rather not bleed into your gin and tonic, get a zester. Remember to zest your fruit right over your drink or glass, so it catches the spritz of oils.

glasses

Let's not get too precious about this. Just because you don't have the right glass doesn't mean you shouldn't mix yourself a drink. But glass sizes and shapes have been perfected over the years to maximize aromas, flavors, and temperatures. When you can, draw on that knowledge and use the appropriate glass for the drink. Have as many of each variety on hand as your lifestyle requires; if you make martinis in batches of 12, have plenty of glasses on hand. And remember, glasses break, so always have a backup.

Cocktail glass
stemmed, conical glass
usually used for martinis
about 6–8 ounces

Old-fashioned glass
short and squat
about 8 ounces

Highball glass
a little taller and less squat
about 8–10 ounces

Collins glass
tall and thin
8–12 ounces

you

Shot glass
duh

need

Pint glass
for beer
16 ounces

Red wineglass
stemmed, wide bowl
about 8–10 ounces, but don't
ever fill it

White wineglass
stemmed, narrower bowl
about 6–8 ounces, but don't
ever fill it

Hurricane
hourglass-shaped, short stem
about 16 ounces

Champagne flute
tall, slim bowl, long stem
about 6–8 ounces

Brandy snifter
wide bowl with small opening, short stem
about 10 ounces, but don't even come close to filling it

Cordial glass
small flute for after dinner drinks, short stem
about 2 ounces

Specialized wineglasses
Pinot Noirs and Cabernets do better in glasses designed specifically for them, but unless you're spending more on wine than rent, don't worry too much about it.

Six Techniques to Master

You'll see showboaty bartenders acting like Tom Cruise in *Cocktail*, and you'll think you'll need to be able to perform the same acrobatics to get a decent mixed drink. You'll be wrong. If you can perform the six actions described in this chapter, you can make any drink in this book. Top tip: Relax. Don't rush when making a drink. Don't lose track of time, but stick with steady, measured motions, and exercise patience and restraint.

Shaking 01

Shaking is meant to quickly cool and mix drinks and also subtly dilute them. Always shake drinks that contain sour mix, like Pisco sours and Tom Collinses, to develop frothiness.

Use your cobbler shaker (see page 39) for shaking. Fill it halfway with large ice cubes (not crushed ice), then pour the ingredients over the top. Shake vigorously. By vigorous, I mean plant your feet, bend your knees slightly, hold the shaker out in front of you with both hands, and shake hard enough to make your face jiggle. You should usually perform this action twice, for about 30 seconds each round with a 30-second rest in between. When beads of condensation have coated the outside of your shaker, you're done.

Stirring 02

Stirring, like shaking, is about cooling and blending your drink, but because less ice melts during the process, stirring dilutes your booze less than shaking. Gin is best stirred because good gin carries a delicate balance of flavors, which can be sensitive to overdilution. So while shaking is fine for relatively flavorless vodka, always stir gin martinis to retain your gin's integrity.

Use your bar glass (or glass half of your Hawthorn shaker) or the base of your cobbler shaker to stir. Stir cocktails more vigorously than you would, say, cream into your coffee, but don't stir hard enough to crack the ice. You can stir 1 drink at a time in a bar glass, or several drinks at once in a pitcher.

Pouring 03

Believe it or not, there's more to pouring than just dumping your drink into a glass. Just like you'd carefully angle a glass at a beer tap to avoid ending up with a head as big as your head, pouring a martini or mixed drink should be done gingerly, introducing as little air as possible into the mix. Leave the unnecessary 4-foot-high cascades to the show-off professionals behind real bars. They've been trained. Keep your rims no more than 6 or 7 inches apart, and never touch your shaker to the side of the glass, as you're likely to break the glass.

Blending 04

Even though the idea of blender drinks makes you think of a big ol' poolside party with half-naked guests gone wild, blender drinks work better with fewer people. Think about it: If you're blending drinks for 36 people, mixing 4–6 drinks at a time, you'll never leave the blender, and no one else will hear the music. Plus, where are you going to keep all that ice? Blender drinks are perfect for 4 people on a porch in the afternoon.

Blending can be tricky business, because if you just let your drink and accompanying ice rip at high speed without paying attention, you'll end up with a pitcher of watered-down booze unfit for consumption by anyone other than a desperate frat boy. Blend in short bursts, or pulses, of no more than 10 or 15 seconds apiece. You can always hit it again if you need to, but once you overblend, your drink is screwed and you have to start over. Oh, and don't overfill your pitcher, or you and your kitchen will be wearing your sticky drink.

Muddling 05

Muddling is used in drinks like mojitos. The idea is to carefully break down things like mint leaves or lime rinds to release the oils, and therefore the flavors, into your glass. Use a firm, but gentle mortar-and-pestle motion, not bashing the hell out of it, but instead gingerly coaxing oils out of the leaves. It's good, when you're muddling, to have an abrasive like sugar or a thick liquid like simple syrup in the glass to speed up the process and also give your muddled oils something to grab onto and dissolve into.

Rolling 06

Rolling a drink, which is what you do for a Bloody Mary, is when you pour it from one glass to another and back. And forth. And back. And forth. The idea is to mix it thoroughly, but not create any foam.

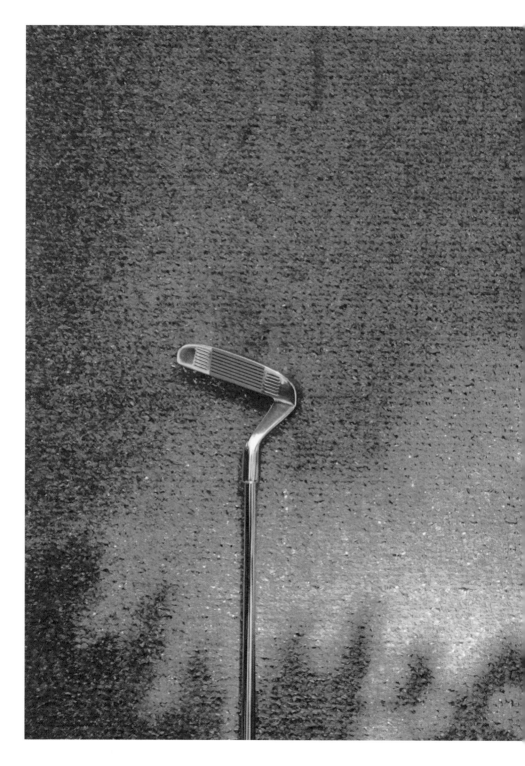

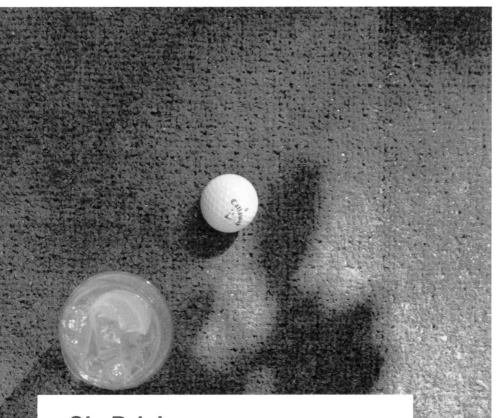

Gin Drinks

A red nose in your old age
is a small price to pay for the occa-
sional nip of gin. We have the
English, excellent drinkers themselves, to thank for the popularity
of herby, bracing gin, which they
drank in copious quantities right
through the Empire's very rise and
fall. My favorite alcohol, especially
when served ice cold.

They never teach you this in Bible class, but at the end of that sixth day, He invented the martini to sip on while He awaited His steak. Hey, it was a long week. The martini is my favorite drink, ever, and always will be. Strong enough to make you wince, but soothing enough to make you melt into your club chair, an icy dry martini occupies not just your throat, but your entire body, as soon as it hits your lips. Instant gratification.

classic martini

INGREDIENTS

2 ounces **gin**, plus 1 splash for luck

½ ounce **dry vermouth**

INSTRUCTIONS

Fill glass with ice water. Set aside. Prepare garnish.

Fill bar glass or shaker base halfway with ice cubes. Add gin and vermouth. Stir gently for 30 seconds, then set aside.

Dump ice water out of glass. Place garnish in glass. Stir gin for 30 seconds more, then strain into glass and sip.

Dirty Martini: Add ½ teaspoon olive juice from the olive jar to the bar glass before the second stir.

Extra-Dry Martini: Instead of adding vermouth to bar glass and stirring with gin, swish vermouth around chilled, empty glass, then dump it and strain in gin.

Gibson: Garnish martini with cocktail onion.

Fifty-Fifty: Up the gin-to-vermouth ratio to 1:1.

Vodka Martini: See page 72.

GLASS

Cocktail, chilled

TIP

Keep your hot, sweaty palms away from the bowl of your glass. They'll heat up your martini and take away its edge. Hold the glass by the stem while you sip.

GARNISH

Your choice: **olive** or twist of **lemon**

gin fizz

MAKES 1 REFRESHING DRINK

INGREDIENTS

Juice of ½ **lemon**, plus
a few gratings of zest

½ ounce **simple syrup**
(page 29)

2 ounces **gin**

Club soda

INSTRUCTIONS

Fill bar glass or shaker base
halfway with ice cubes. Add
lemon juice, lemon zest, simple
syrup, and gin. Stir gently for
30 seconds, then set aside.

Fill glass three-quarters full with
ice cubes. Stuff lemon round
down into glass, alongside ice.
Stir gin mixture for 30 seconds
more, then strain into glass. Fill
remainder of glass with club
soda and stir gently. Serve.

GARNISH

Thin lemon round

GLASS

Highball

VARIATION

Ginger Gin Fizz: Use ginger
ale *(regular, not diet)* instead
of club soda.

Fresca Fizz: Skip the powdered
sugar and use Fresca
(original, not peach) instead
of club soda.

Ritzy Fizz: Substitute Champagne or another sparkling
wine for club soda.

TIP

Save your very best gin for martinis. Use the second-shelf stuff
here, especially if you're dabbling
in one of the variations down
there at the bottom.

Where mint juleps are a porch drink, gin fizzes are
a deck drink, best enjoyed near a body of water, or
better yet, on the back of a boat around dusk, with
your line in the lake and no expectations.

gin rickey

2 ounces **gin**

Juice of ½ **lime**

Club soda

Fill glass halfway full with ice cubes. Add gin and lime juice. Fill with club soda and stir gently. Garnish with lime wedge and serve.

Lime wedge

Highball

Frozen Rickey: Combine ingredients in a blender with 1½ cups crushed ice. Blend for 10 seconds, pulsing in additional 5-second increments if necessary, then serve immediately.

Sweet Rickey: Add 1–2 ounces simple syrup *(page 29)*.

Cherry Rickey: Use equal parts marinated cherry juice and lime juice.

Don't overdo it on the syrup. A rickey should be zingy, not sticky.

MAKES **1** RICKEY

Rickeys come in all varieties, from boozy to benign, from bourbon to vodka. But the best version is the classic gin rickey. Serve rickeys in the afternoon, in your backyard or someone else's.

2   ounces **gin**

½ ounce **Cointreau**

Juice of ½ **lime**

Juice of ½ **lemon**

Splash of **water**

Dash of **bitters**

Fill bar glass or shaker base halfway with ice cubes. Add all ingredients and stir gently for 30 seconds. Set aside.

Fill glass halfway with ice cubes. Stir gin mixture for 30 seconds more, then strain into glass. Top with orange twist and cherry and serve.

MAKES **1** SLURRED-SPEECH-INDUCING SLING

Slings are meant to be drunk late in the afternoon, preferably during a tropical rainstorm. But there's no reason they can't be drunk in the evening, before dinner. Or for that matter, during a long Wednesday lunch when the boss is away on business.

Orange twist

Maraschino cherry

Old-fashioned

Pineapple Sling: Substitute about 1 ounce pineapple juice for lime and lemon juice, and use a pineapple wedge for garnish.

Lady Sling: Add ½ ounce cherry brandy and 2 drops grenadine to the mix.

Frozen Sling: Combine ingredients in a blender with 1 cup crushed ice. Blend for 10 seconds, pulsing in additional 5-second increments if necessary, and serve in hurricane glass.

When I say a splash of water, I mean it. Don't add any more than 1 tablespoon.

1½ ounces **gin**

1 ounce **Campari**

1 ounce **sweet vermouth**

Fill bar glass or shaker base halfway with ice cubes. Add gin, Campari, and vermouth. Stir gently for 30 seconds.

Strain gin mixture into glass. Garnish and sip.

MAKES **1** CLASSY DRINK

negroni

Where most gin drinks go sweet somewhere along the way, a negroni is bitter, puckering, and totally addictive. This Italian take on gin was invented as an aperitif, to stimulate the appetite before a gargantuan Italian meal. But I think it's at its best outdoors, in the afternoon. Wear sunglasses and throw attitude while you sip.

Orange twist

Cocktail

Negroni Rocks: Use highball glass. Fill glass halfway with ice, add garnish, and strain mixture over the top.

Licorice Negroni: Substitute Pernod or pastis for the Campari.

Chill your ingredients for an hour before mixing for a less-diluted negroni.

2 ounces **gin**

½ ounce fresh **lime** juice

½ teaspoon **simple syrup**
   (page 29)

Fill bar glass or shaker base halfway with ice cubes. Add gin, lime juice, and simple syrup and stir gently for 30 seconds.

Place lime round in bottom of glass. Add 2 ice cubes. Strain gin mixture into glass, garnish, and serve.

Even though a gimlet is really just a jacked-up martini, there's something about the addition of lime and sugar that makes it seem, well, less alcoholic. Don't be fooled. One of these babies will have you begging for another, and two will have you begging for mercy.

classic gimlet

MAKES **1** TASTY GIMLET

Lime round

Lime twist

Old-fashioned

VARIATIONS

Gimlet Up: Strain ingredients into a chilled cocktail glass.

Frozen Gimlet: Combine ingredients in a blender. Use a squeeze or 2 more of lime juice. Add 1 cup crushed ice. Blend for 10 seconds, pulsing in additional 5-second increments if necessary, then serve.

Fizzy Gimlet: Use a Tom Collins glass, pour gin mixture over ice cubes, and add club soda to fill.

TIP

Use a lighter-flavored gin with this drink, like Bombay Sapphire. And don't overstir it. Save the more botanical Tanqueray for your martinis.

Splash of **dry vermouth**

Splash of **sweet vermouth**

2   ounces **gin**

Juice of 1 **orange**

Splash of **simple syrup**
*(optional, depending on how
sweet your orange is; page 29)*

Fill bar glass or shaker base
halfway with ice cubes. Add
vermouths, gin, orange juice,
and simple syrup and stir gently
for 30 seconds. Set aside.

Place 4 ice cubes in glass. Stir
gin mixture for 30 seconds more,
then strain into glass. Garnish
with orange round and serve.

GARNISH

Orange round

GLASS

Old-fashioned

VARIATIONS

Bronx Cherry: Use cherry
    brandy instead of sweet
    vermouth.

South Bronx: Use only 1 ounce
    of gin and add 1 ounce sloe
    gin.

TIP

Squeeze fresh juice for this one.
Don't use orange juice from the
fridge, or you'll wonder what the
big deal about a Bronx cocktail is.

**Some people say the Bronx Cocktail was first mixed
in Manhattan,** others say Philadelphia. Hardly anyone
believes it was invented in the Bronx. Just don't say
that too loud in the wrong neighborhood.

MAKES **1** COCKTAIL

bronx
cocktail

salty dog

INGREDIENTS

2 ounces **gin**

6 ounces **grapefruit juice** *(fresh if possible)*, pulp strained out

INSTRUCTIONS

Fill cocktail shaker halfway with ice cubes. Add gin and grapefruit juice. Shake gently for 30 seconds.

Rim glass with salt *(see page 35)*. Fill glass halfway with ice cubes. Shake cocktail 15 more seconds, then strain into glass, being careful not to damage the salt rim. Garnish with lime twist and serve.

GARNISHES

Fine salt for rimming glass

Lime twist

GLASS

Highball

VARIATIONS

Florida Dog: Use a half-and-half mixture of orange and grapefruit juice.

Tropical Dog: Use pineapple juice instead of grapefruit juice.

TIP

Use less salt than you would for a margarita.

They say a sprinkle of salt on your morning grapefruit half really enhances the flavor. Same goes for this salty old drink—the grapefruit explodes against that salty rim. One too many of these makes sea dogs, and landlubbers, howl and bay at the moon. A great fishing drink.

INGREDIENTS

2 ounces **gin**

½ ounce **Pernod**

INSTRUCTIONS

Fill cocktail shaker halfway with ice cubes. Add gin and Pernod. Stir vigorously for 30 seconds. Set aside.

Fill glass halfway with crushed ice. Stir gin mixture for 30 seconds more, then strain into glass and garnish with lemon twist. Serve.

GARNISH

Lemon twist

GLASS

Old-fashioned

VARIATIONS

Absinthe Fog: Use absinthe instead of Pernod. *(Some would say this is more traditional.)*

Lemon Fog: Use Limoncello instead of Pernod.

TIP

This is a foggy drink. Pernod *(like other licorice liqueurs)* becomes cloudy when it's stirred with ice.

MAKES **1** DRINK *(HAVE 2, AND YOU'LL BE THE FOGGY ONE)*

There is no flavor on the planet quite like licorice, and there's no better showcase for it than in a drink. While I enjoy a chilly Pernod on the rocks just by itself *(a pleasure I was first introduced to by my friend Pete, who also happens to know everything about steak, making him a good friend indeed)*, this is my favorite way to drink the stuff.

There are as many stories about the history of the Tom Collins as there are bars in the civilized world. If you're a West Coast drinker, you probably believe it was invented in San Francisco. If you're a New Yorker, this is a New York drink all the way. Even the Australians have local-origin myths concerning the Collins. Whatever. Have a couple, then discuss among yourselves.

MAKES **1** PERFECT DRINK

tom

2½ ounces **gin**

1 ounce **sour mix** *(page 29)*

Club soda

Fill bar glass or shaker base halfway with ice cubes. Add gin and sour mix. Shake for 30 seconds. Set aside.

Place 2 or 3 ice cubes in glass. Add orange round. Shake gin mixture for 30 seconds, then strain into glass. Top with club soda. Garnish with cherry and serve.

Orange round

Maraschino cherry

Collins, genius

Whiskey Collins: Use bourbon or rye whiskey instead of gin.

Rum Collins: Use rum instead of gin.

Look for a frothy top to this drink. If there's no froth, just fizz, it's not a Tom Collins.

collins

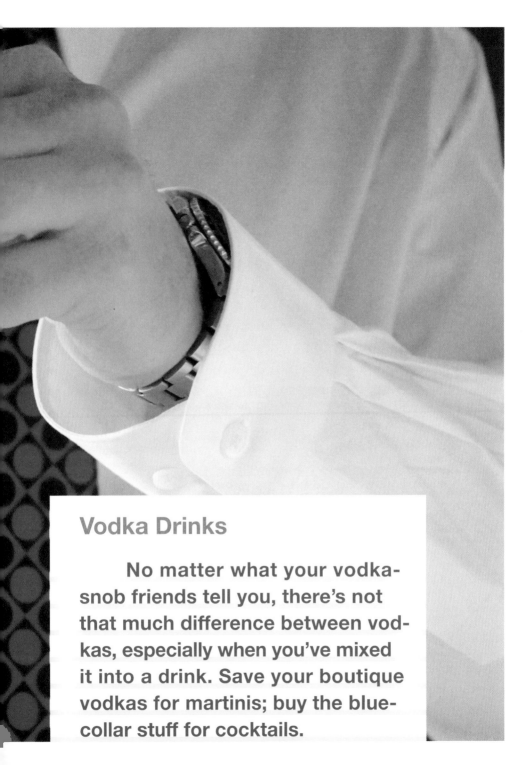

Vodka Drinks

No matter what your vodka-snob friends tell you, there's not that much difference between vodkas, especially when you've mixed it into a drink. Save your boutique vodkas for martinis; buy the blue-collar stuff for cocktails.

Fill glass with ice water. Set aside. Prepare garnish.

Fill cocktail shaker halfway with ice cubes. Add vodka and vermouth. Cap shaker and shake gently for 20 seconds.

Dump ice water out of glass. Place garnish in glass, shake drink gently for 20 seconds, then strain in martini. Serve immediately.

INGREDIENTS

2 ounces **vodka**

½ ounce **dry vermouth**

Most dedicated gin drinkers pooh-pooh the vodka martini, but I, a fairly dedicated gin drinker myself, don't. Vodka, treated correctly, is crisp and clean in a way that hoary old gin could never be, and for reasons I can't explain, a fresh vodka martini always seems colder than gin. And besides, those Russians, who invented the stuff, are no slackers when it comes to booze.

vodka

GARNISH

Martini olive or **lemon** twist

GLASS

Cocktail, chilled

VARIATIONS

Dirty Martini: Add a spoonful of olive juice to the shaker.

Vodka Gibson: Use a cocktail onion instead of olive or twist.

Gin Martini: See page 54.

TIP

Unlike a gin martini, you can shake the hell out of vodka. Just don't overdo it, or you'll have too many floaters *(bits of ice)* in your drink.

MAKES **1** BOND-WORTHY COCKTAIL

martini

vodka gimlet

Traditional gimlets are made with gin *(see page 62)*, but over the last few decades or so, vodka gimlets have become more common. Because of the bright green color and tart lime taste, you'll fool yourself into thinking that you're having a relatively tame mixed drink. Until you try to stand up.

INGREDIENTS

2 ½ ounces **vodka**

Juice of ½ **lime**

1   teaspoon **simple syrup** *(page 29)*

GARNISH

Lime round

VARIATIONS

Lemon-Lime Gimlet: Add a squirt of fresh lemon juice to the mix. Garnish with lemon twist.

Fizzy Gimlet: Add a splash of soda water.

Cucumber Gimlet: Crush ½ cucumber and add it to the cocktail shaker when shaking. Garnish with 1 lime round and 1 cucumber round.

Classic Gin Gimlet: See page 62.

INSTRUCTIONS

Fill cocktail shaker halfway with ice cubes. Add vodka, lime juice, and simple syrup. Shake gently for 60 seconds. Set aside.

Place lime round in bottom of glass. Shake vodka mixture for 30 seconds more, then strain into glass and serve.

GLASS

Cocktail, chilled

TIP

Operate heavy machinery at your own risk. Better yet, find someone else to do it for you.

Nothing, except maybe a Bloody Mary *(page 76)*, says "Good morning" like a screwdriver. But orange juice isn't just for breakfast anymore, so buck the trend and have this for lunch.

screwdriver

INGREDIENTS

Juice of 2 **oranges** *(about 4–6 ounces)*

2   ounces **vodka**

Dash of **bitters**

GARNISH

Lime wedge

INSTRUCTIONS

Place a few rocks in your glass. Add orange juice, vodka, and bitters to glass, in that order. Stir, garnish, and serve.

MAKES **1** GOOD SCREW

VARIATIONS

Frozen Screw: Combine orange juice, vodka, bitters, and 1 cup crushed ice in a blender and blend for 10 seconds, pulsing in additional 5-second increments if necessary. Pour into glass, garnish with lime wedge, and serve.

Classy Screw: Substitute 1 ounce Cointreau for 1 ounce of the vodka.

Fizzy Screw: Use just 4 ounces of orange juice. Skip the blender. Add ingredients to highball glass with a few rocks, then fill glass with Orangina.

GLASS

Highball

TIP

Try this drink with different bitters—Angostura, Peychaud's, orange. Find the one you like and stick with it.

5 ounces **tomato juice**

1 ounce **Clamato juice**

2 dashes of **Worcestershire sauce**

3 or 4 dashes of **Tabasco sauce**

¼ teaspoon **prepared horseradish**

Pinch of **celery salt**

2 ounces **vodka**

INSTRUCTIONS

In bar glass or shaker base, combine all ingredients except vodka. Roll drink by pouring it into another bar glass, then back, then forth, then back. Taste and adjust seasonings.

Add 6 ice cubes to glass. Pour in vodka, then top with bloody mix. Stir with celery stalk, then garnish with the celery, lime wedge, and olive and serve.

MAKES **1** HANGOVER CURE

There are more recipes for Bloody Marys than almost any other cocktail. I recently was at a restaurant that used au jus from their French Dip sandwiches in theirs, and it wasn't bad. Anyway, here's my favorite version. Don't worry, Clamato juice doesn't make it taste fishy, just good.

Celery stalk

Lime wedge

Olive

Highball or **Collins**

Jalapeño Mary: Replace horseradish and Tabasco sauce with ¼ teaspoon minced jalapeño.

Swedish Mary: Replace celery salt with dried dill.

Bloody Maria: Replace vodka with white tequila, and add a few squeezes of fresh lemon juice to the mix.

Serve this spicy drink with a glass of water on the side.

cape codder

INGREDIENTS

6 ounces **cranberry juice**

2 ounces **vodka**

Juice of ½ **lime**

INSTRUCTIONS

Fill bar glass or shaker base half-way with ice cubes. Add cranberry juice, vodka, and lime juice. Stir gently for 30 seconds.

Fill glass halfway with ice cubes. Strain cocktail over glass, garnish, and serve.

GARNISH

Lime wedge

GLASS

Highball

VARIATIONS

Frozen Cod: Combine all ingredients in a blender with 1½ cups crushed ice. Blend for 10 seconds, pulsing in additional 5-second increments if necessary. Pour into glasses, garnish with lime wedges, and serve in a hurricane glass.

Fizzy Cod: Use 4 ounces cranberry juice, and top off with club soda.

TIP

Don't try to squeeze juice out of cranberries. Just use the stuff in the bottle.

If there's any part of the country where the people know how to drink, it's Cape Cod, Massachusetts. All summer long it's a big resort, where the cocktails flow freely. And all winter? It's got some of the toughest weather in the world, windy and snowy and wet. Makes me want a drink just thinking about it.

We can thank California for many things: **Surfing culture, the Red Hot Chili Peppers, the odd gold rush. And, indeed, the Harvey Wallbanger. Whether it was actually named after a dude named Harvey or not remains a story destined for the hazy fog of cocktail history.**

INGREDIENTS

2 ounces **vodka**

½ ounce **Galliano liqueur**

Juice of 2 **oranges**

INSTRUCTIONS

Place 5 or 6 ice cubes in glass. Add vodka, then Galliano, and stir. Top with orange juice and stir again. Garnish with orange round and serve.

GARNISH

Orange round

GLASS

Highball or **Collins**

VARIATION

Frozen Bang: Combine ingredients with 2 cups crushed ice in blender. Blend for 15 seconds, pulsing in additional 5-second increments if necessary. Garnish and serve.

TIP

Don't overmix this drink.

MAKES **1** BANGER

harvey wallbanger

INGREDIENTS

4   ounces **vodka**

    Juice of 2 **lemons**

1   ounce **simple syrup**
    (page 29), or more if your
    lemons are especially sour

INSTRUCTIONS

Rim glasses with sugar
(see page 35).

Place all ingredients in blender,
then add 2 cups crushed ice.
Blend for 10 seconds, pulsing in
additional 5-second increments
if necessary. Pour into glasses,
being careful not to disturb
sugar rims, and garnish with lemon
twist. Serve immediately.

THESE ARE BEST SHARED, SO THIS RECIPE

MAKES 2 DROPS

On the coldest day of the year, feel free to turn up the heat in your house, throw on your flip-flops, and mix a couple of these babies in front of an old Elvis movie. You'll remember what July feels like soon enough.

GARNISHES

Sugar for rimming glasses

Lemon twists

GLASS

Margarita

VARIATIONS

Classic Lemon Drop: Forget the blender. Use a highball glass, pouring all ingredients over rocks.

Cherry Drop: Add a splash of grenadine, and garnish with a maraschino cherry.

Rum Drop: Substitute rum for vodka.

TIP

Don't use your best vodka on these. Save your fancy brands for your straight martinis.

frozen lemon drop

2   ounces **vodka**

1   ounce **Cointreau**

Juice of ½ **lime**

Splash of **simple syrup**
(page 29)

Fill cocktail shaker halfway with ice cubes. Add vodka, Cointreau, lime juice, and simple syrup. Stir gently for 30 seconds.

Wring lime twist over glass to release oils, then drop twist into glass. Strain drink into glass and serve.

GARNISH

Lime twist

GLASS

Cocktail, chilled

VARIATIONS

Blue 'kaze: Use blue curaçao instead of Cointreau.

Pink 'kaze: Substitute cranberry juice for lime juice. Garnish with a maraschino cherry.

TIP

Stir this one, don't shake.

Much like a margarita, only using vodka rather than tequila, the kamikaze is a deceptively smooth drink. Two of these suckers, and you'll be yelling, "Banzai!" Hopefully you won't be streaking through the neighborhood at the time like I was. Just kidding. No, really—just kidding.

kamikaze

MAKES **1** DRINK

IRRESPONSIBLY ALCOHOLIC

MAKES

2

FROGGY DRINKS

frozen bullfrog

5   ounces **vodka**

2   tablespoons **frozen limeade concentrate**

2   tablespoons chilled **heavy cream**

Place 2 cups crushed ice in blender. Add vodka and lime-ade concentrate. Blend for 10 seconds. Add cream. Blend for 5 seconds, pulsing in additional 5-second increments if necessary. Pour into glasses, garnish with lime wedges, and serve immediately.

GARNISH

Lime wedges

GLASS

Cocktail or **old-fashioned**

VARIATION

Classic Bullfrog: Stir together 2 ounces vodka and 6 ounces limeade. Pour into rocks-filled old-fashioned glass and stir. Garnish with lime wedge.

TIP

Make sure your cream is cold. Put it in the freezer for a half hour if necessary before blending.

Like a lime-sicle in a glass, **this summertime cooler is creamy and smooth. Serve these in the afternoon, when you're lying around in the sun by the pool. Or in front of the television, your choice.**

½ ounce **vodka**

½ ounce **gin**

½ ounce **tequila**

½ ounce **dark rum**

½ ounce **light rum**

½ ounce **Cointreau**

2 ounces **sour mix** *(page 29)*

4 ounces **Coca-Cola**

Fill bar glass or shaker base halfway with ice cubes. Add all ingredients except Coca-Cola. Stir gently for 30 seconds.

Place 4 or 5 ice cubes in glass. Strain cocktail mixture into glass, then top with Coke and stir. Garnish with lime round and cherry and serve immediately.

The classic kitchen-sink cocktail *(i.e., you put into it everything* but*)*, the Long Island Iced Tea has long been a favorite of lush-living ladies who lunch and the tennis pros who love them. It'd be wrong to serve this drink without collecting keys from your guests first. You can mix these by the pitcher, but if you do, plan to provide buckets to passed-out guests.

long island

MAKES 1 ABSURDLY BOOZY DRINK

GARNISHES

Lime round

Maraschino cherry

GLASS

Collins

VARIATIONS

Diet Long Island Iced Tea:
Substitute Diet Coke
for Coke.

Peach Long Island Iced Tea:
Substitute peach schnapps
for Cointreau.

Cherry Long Island Iced Tea:
Substitute Heering cherry
liqueur or kirsch for Cointreau.

TIP

Don't worry too hard if you don't
have all the ingredients. You
can jazz these with pretty much
whatever's in your cupboard.

iced tea

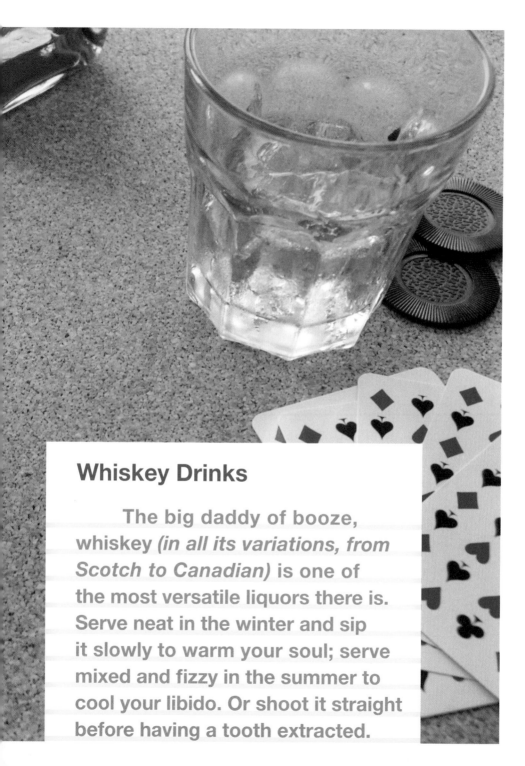

Whiskey Drinks

The big daddy of booze, whiskey *(in all its variations, from Scotch to Canadian)* is one of the most versatile liquors there is. Serve neat in the winter and sip it slowly to warm your soul; serve mixed and fizzy in the summer to cool your libido. Or shoot it straight before having a tooth extracted.

manhattan

INGREDIENTS

2 ounces **rye whiskey**

½ ounce **sweet vermouth**

1 dash of **Angostura bitters**

INSTRUCTIONS

Fill bar glass or shaker base halfway with ice cubes. Add whiskey and vermouth. Stir gently for **30** seconds.

Place cherry in bottom of glass. Rub lemon twist around rim of glass to impart its oils to the rim, then drop it in. Strain cocktail into glass and serve.

GARNISHES

Maraschino cherry

Lemon twist

GLASS

Cocktail, chilled

VARIATIONS

Uptown Manhattan: Substitute brandy for whiskey.

Manhattan Lady: Add ½ ounce Dubonnet Rouge to mix.

TIP

If you can't find rye whiskey *(see page 14)* in your liquor cabinet, any blended whiskey will do.

Little more than a martini made with whiskey, the Manhattan is a great equalizing drink, equally at home in the most elegant wood-paneled country club as in the seediest of alleyway bars. This is the kind of drink that makes you tell stories you'd otherwise pack away at the back of your brain, so be careful who you drink this with. Expect to feel it tomorrow, but sometimes that's half the fun of drinking.

INGREDIENTS

3 ounces **Canadian**
   or **bourbon whiskey**

1½ ounces **sour mix** *(page 29)*

INSTRUCTIONS

Fill cocktail shaker halfway with
ice cubes. Add whiskey and
sour mix. Shake vigorously for
60 seconds.

Drop cherry into glass, then give
whiskey mixture a final shake and
strain it over the top.

GARNISH

Maraschino cherry

GLASS

Ideally, you'd serve this
in a **sour glass.** But a **white
wineglass** will work.

VARIATIONS

Gramp's Sour: Use Fresca
   instead of sour mix.

Fizzy Sour: Use a highball glass,
   and top off with club soda.

TIP

Use good whiskey, but not the
best whiskey.

My grandfather used to make whiskey sours in the
summertime, using Fresca instead of sour mix. They
were delicious, especially with Spanish peanuts. Mine
are a little more traditional, using sour mix instead of
Fresca.

MAKES **1** DRINK, BEST CONSUMED IN THE AFTERNOON

thirsty

2 ounces **bourbon**

Juice of ½ **lemon**

1 splash **Peychaud's bitters**

7UP

Fill bar glass or shaker base halfway with ice cubes. Add bourbon and lemon juice. Stir for 30 seconds, then set aside.

Place orange peel in bottom of glass. Add a few cubes of ice. Stir bourbon mixture for 30 more seconds, then strain into glass. Top with 7UP and serve.

No one enjoys his Beam and Seven more than my friend Andy Fishering, a savant when it comes to eye-balling proportions of bourbon to mixer. This libation, a bastardization of the clear-as-mud mixture he usually fixes (just Beam and Seven, no lemon, no garnish), is tough enough to serve to the boys, but plenty girly for the ladies, too.

fish

QUENCHING COCKTAIL

GARNISH

Orange peel *(use a vegetable peeler and make it about 1 inch wide and 2–3 inches long)*

VARIATIONS

Thirsty Girl Fish: Add ½ ounce grenadine.

Smoky Fish: Light a long kitchen match. Pass orange peel over flame, twisting to spritz oils from the peel into the flame. Do this over the glass so that the flamed oil lands in the glass. *(Tip: Have a friend hold the match.)*

GLASS

Highball

TIP

Don't use Jack Daniel's here. Not that there's anything wrong with Jack Daniel's, but it's better in a whiskey sour.

mint julep

The nice thing about serving mint juleps on Kentucky Derby day is that they last all afternoon, while the race itself is over in about six seconds. The not-nice thing about serving them on Derby day is, if you have more than one before the start gun goes off, you're likely to miss the race because you had to go pee.

MAKES **1** HORSE RACE–WORTHY DRINK

INGREDIENTS

1 small **mint sprig** for muddling

1 teaspoon **simple syrup** *(page 29)*

2½ ounces **bourbon**

GARNISHES

Sugar for rimming glass

Mint sprig

INSTRUCTIONS

Place 1 mint sprig and simple syrup in bottom of glass. Muddle *(see page 50)*. Rim glass with sugar *(see page 35)*, being careful not to pour out muddled mint. Fill glass with crushed ice. Add bourbon to glass and stir well. Garnish with mint sprig and serve.

GLASS

Old-fashioned

VARIATIONS

Orange Julep: Substitute 1 ounce fresh orange juice for the simple syrup, and garnish with an orange twist.

TIP

Use crushed ice in these, not big cubes.

Orange round

Dash of **Peychaud's bitters**

1 sugar cube

2 ounces **bourbon**

Splash of **club soda**

Place orange round, bitters, and sugar cube in glass. Muddle *(see page 50)*. Add 4 ice cubes. Add bourbon, then top with club soda. Stir. Garnish with cherry and serve.

If I had a wood-paneled library with an oversized club chair and an hour to kill before dinner, I'd have an old-fashioned. Then again, even though I have no wood paneling, I'll still take the drink. This is an excellent drink to mix for yourself. Not that I'm suggesting drinking alone, but, well, if you're going to drink alone, this is a good way to do it.

GARNISHES

Maraschino cherry

GLASS

Old-fashioned, duh

VARIATIONS

Flat Old-fashioned: Substitute water for club soda.

Irish Old-fashioned: Substitute Irish whiskey for bourbon.

Italian Old-fashioned: Substitute Campari for Peychaud's.

TIP

Assemble this drink in the order suggested; don't just toss it all in a glass. It may make the drink taste better, or it may not, but it's tradition, dammit.

MAKES **1** CLASSY COCKTAIL

2   ounces **Scotch**

Splash of **sweet vermouth**

Splash of **dry vermouth**

GARNISHES

Lemon twist

Maraschino cherry

INSTRUCTIONS

Fill bar glass or shaker base half-way with ice cubes. Add Scotch and vermouths. Stir gently for 30 seconds. Set aside.

Add 3 or 4 ice cubes to glass, then twist lemon over the top to release oils into the glass and drop in lemon twist. Stir the whisky mixture for 15 seconds more, then strain into glass. Garnish with cherry and serve.

GLASS

Old-fashioned

VARIATIONS

Dry Roy: Use only dry vermouth.

Sweet Boy Roy: Use only sweet vermouth.

Manhattan Roy: Add a few drops of Angostura bitters.

TIP

Don't use the best Scotch in the house for this one. Save the boutique single-malt for sipping, and reach to the second shelf when mixing Rob Roys.

The Rob Roy should be near the top of the "endangered cocktails" list. No one orders them anymore. This is a shame, because this bracing brew is one of the finest around. Make it your duty to serve them at home, and order them out.

rob roy

MAKES **1** DRINK, GUARANTEED TO BLOW YOUR KILT UP

2 FROZEN COFFEES

It sucked to live in the old days, when coffee came only one way: hot. Like it or not, we live in a frappuccino nation these days, to which I say, if you can't lick 'em, fire up the blender and join 'em.

frozen irish coffee

INGREDIENTS

3 ounces **Irish whiskey**

1 cup cold **double-strength coffee** *(brew it twice as strong, then chill it)*

2 ounces **simple syrup**

2 ounces **half-and-half**

INSTRUCTIONS

Rim mugs with brown sugar *(see page 35)*.

Combine whiskey, coffee, simple syrup, and half-and-half in a blender with 2 cups crushed ice. Blend for 10 seconds, pulsing in additional 5-second increments if necessary. Pour into mugs and serve with straws.

Brown sugar for rimming
   glasses

Beer mug, chilled

Classic Irish Coffee: Use hot
   coffee at regular strength.
   Mix all ingredients in coffee
   mug, then top with dollop
   of whipped cream.

Irish Mint Coffee: Add 1 ounce
   crème de menthe to the mix.

Serve in cold glasses so your drink
stays colder longer. Therefore,
keep your glasses in the freezer.

Rum Drinks

Short of commandeering a yacht and island-hopping along the Dry Tortugas, rum is the best way to unleash your inner pirate. There are a million brands on the market, so buy lots of little bottles and taste-test them. And for my money, flavored rums just aren't worth it. Yo-ho-ho.

3 ounces **light rum**

Juice of 2 **limes**

1 teaspoon **simple syrup**
   (page 29)

Fill cocktail shaker halfway with ice cubes. Add rum and lime juice. Shake vigorously for 60 seconds. Set aside.

Place lime round in bottom of glass. Add simple syrup and muddle *(see page 50)*.

Add 3 ice cubes to glass. Shake rum mixture for 30 more seconds, then strain into glass and serve.

GARNISH

Lime round

GLASS

Old-fashioned

VARIATIONS

Winter Daiquiri: Add 2 ounces of Cointreau to the mix, and garnish with orange instead of lime.

Red Daiquiri: Substitute Grenadine for lime juice, and garnish with a slice of lemon instead of lime.

Frozen Daiquiri: See page 104.

TIP

Sip, don't chug.

MAKES 1 DRINK THAT DESERVES TO BE SIPPED IN BARBADOS, BUT BUFFALO WILL DO

classic daiquiri

There is something to be said about an icy frozen blender daiquiri, but we'll say it later. For now, let's focus on the classic daiquiri, the kind that Hemingway threw back with abandon after overfishing the Keys. Many bars serve their daiquiris shaken and strained, like a martini, but I prefer mine in a highball glass with a few rocks and a circle of lime. I also like dark rum, usually. Try several rums before you settle on a favorite; they're as varied as whiskeys or Scotches.

6   ounces **white rum**

⅓ cup **limeade concentrate**

2   ounces **Cointreau**

2   tablespoons **simple syrup**
    (page 29), or to taste

Up to an hour before you mix these, rinse 4 hurricane glasses in cold water. Don't dry them off, just place them in the freezer to chill.

Remove glasses from freezer. Combine rum, limeade, Cointreau, and simple syrup in a blender. Add about 4 cups of crushed ice. Blend for 15 seconds, pulsing in additional 5-second increments if necessary.

Divide daiquiri evenly between glasses. Garnish with lime wedge. *(This garnish is not just for show. When you serve these, make sure you squeeze the lime over the top . . . it really adds a nice bite.)*

If the margarita is the queen of frozen drinks, the daiquiri is the king. Think of this recipe as a base, to which you should add any and all flavors you can imagine, from mint to pineapple to cinnamon.

MAKES **1**

BLENDERFUL OF DAIQUIRIS, ENOUGH FOR ABOUT 4 LARGE DRINKS

Lime wedges

Hurricane

Strawberry Daiquiri: Use half as much limeade and add a handful of fresh or frozen strawberries to the blender.

Peach Frozen Daiquiri: Skip the limeade, and drop in a couple pitted, cubed, and frozen peaches or 1 cup of prefrozen peaches.

If you have leftovers in your blender, use them quick. Always top off your drink before you finish it, or those leftovers will just melt.

frozen daiquiri

2 ounces **dark rum**

½ ounce **Cointreau**

Juice of ½ **lime**

Splash of **orgeat syrup***
or **amaretto liqueur**

*Look for orgeat syrup,
an almond-flavored syrup,
at an import store like
Trader Joe's or World Market.

INSTRUCTIONS

Fill cocktail shaker halfway
with ice cubes. Add ingredients
and shake gently for 30 seconds. Place lime round in bottom
of glass. Add 3 ice cubes to
glass. Shake cocktail for 30 seconds more, then strain into glass.
Garnish with cherry and mint
and serve.

MAKES **1**
INSTANT-VACATION DRINK

classic mai tai

The Mai Tai is my third favorite cocktail in the world,
after a good old martini and a deftly built negroni. They
say that Victor Bergeron *(a.k.a. Trader Vic)* invented
this cocktail back in the 1940s. If they're right, I say
the man deserved a nod from the Nobel Committee.

Lime round

Maraschino cherry

Mint sprig

Hurricane

Frozen Mai Tai: Quadruple recipe, then combine rum, Cointreau, lime juice, and orgeat in a blender with 4 cups crushed ice. Blend for 10 seconds, pulsing in additional 5-second intervals if necessary. Pour into glasses, garnish with cherries and mint, and serve. Serves four.

Orange Tai: Add the juice of 1 orange to the mix.

Got decorative umbrellas? Get 'em out.

mojito

2 **mint sprigs**

Juice of 1 **lime**

1 ounce **simple syrup** *(page 29)*

2 ounces **white rum**

A few drops **Angostura bitters**

4 ounces **club soda**

Place 2 mint sprigs and lime juice in bottom of glass. Muddle *(see page 50)* to bruise the mint leaves. Add simple syrup and muddle a little more.

Place 3 ice cubes in glass, then add rum. Drop in bitters, then top with club soda. Garnish with lime wedge and mint sprig and serve immediately.

GARNISHES

Lime wedge

Mint sprig

GLASS

Highball

VARIATIONS

Millionaire's Mojito: Substitute Champagne for club soda.

Lemon-jito: Substitute lemon juice for lime.

TIP

Take it easy on the muddling, chief. You want to ease those mint oils out of the leaves, not bash the bejesus out of them.

Mojitos, long served in Miami, started trickling into the rest of the country in the late 1990s and are now served in almost every bar in America. I, for one, am thankful.

MAKES **1** SUMMERY MOJITO

There are those people out there for whom it's just not a party without a frozen piña colada. Most of them also sailed on the Love Boat back in the 1970s. But hey, I loved *The Love Boat*, and I love a frozen piña. Bottoms up.

INGREDIENTS

- 2 ounces **white rum**
- 2 ounces **dark rum**
- 3 ounces **pineapple juice**
- 2 ounces **Coco Lopez coconut cream**

INSTRUCTIONS

Pour rums, pineapple juice, and coconut cream into blender. Add 3 cups crushed ice. Blend for 10 seconds, pulsing in additional 5-second increments if necessary. Pour, garnish with pineapple wedge, and serve.

GARNISH

Pineapple wedge

GLASS

Hurricane

VARIATIONS

Classic Colada: Fill bar glass or shaker base halfway with ice cubes. Add 1 ounce white rum, 1 ounce dark rum, 2 ounces each pineapple juice and Coco Lopez cream. Stir gently for 60 seconds, then strain into old-fashioned glasses with a few rocks.

Coffee-Colada: Add 1 ounce Kahlúa to the mix.

TIP

Go for Coco Lopez coconut cream in this recipe. I don't know what they put in it, but it sure is good.

MAKES **2** DRINKS

frozen piña colada

2 ounces **dark rum**

2 ounces **light rum**

1 ounce **cherry brandy**

1 ounce **Cointreau**

2 ounces **sour mix**
(page 29)

4 ounces **freshly squeezed
orange juice** (about
2 oranges)

Fill cocktail shaker halfway with ice cubes. Add all ingredients except orange juice. Shake vigorously for 30 seconds.

Fill glasses halfway with crushed ice. Add orange juice to shaker and stir until combined. Strain into glasses.

Gently pour ¼ ounce 151-proof rum into each drink, pouring it over the back of an overturned spoon held just millimeters from surface of drink so it floats on top. Garnish with orange wedge and serve.

ZOMBIES SHOULD NEVER BE DRUNK ALONE, SO THIS RECIPE MAKES

2 COMA-INDUCING DRINKS

Here's an example of a drink whose sole reason for being is to get the drinker as drunk as possible, as quickly as possible. Too sweet for everyday drinking, this is a good one for parties. Just have the number for a taxi posted at the exit.

½ ounce **151-proof rum**
for floating

Orange wedges

Pacific Zombie: Substitute
pineapple juice for orange
juice.

Pink Zombie: Add 2 splashes
of grenadine.

Frozen Zombie: Combine all
ingredients except floater and
garnish in a blender. Add
2 cups crushed ice. Blend for
10 seconds, pulsing in additional 5-second increments
if necessary. Garnish, pour,
drink, pass out.

Highball

Skip the floater if you plan to
stay up for the good part of the
evening.

1 gallon **apple cider**

2 small **oranges**

12 **cloves**

4 **cinnamon sticks**

1 teaspoon **allspice**

   A few gratings of **nutmeg**

12 ounces **dark rum**

Pour cider into large saucepan.
Stud oranges with 6 cloves each,
then halve oranges and add to
cider. Drop in cinnamon sticks,
allspice, and nutmeg. Heat
slowly to a low simmer.

Pour about 1½ ounces rum into
each mug. Place orange round in
mug. Ladle in spiced cider to fill.
Serve hot.

hot apple

THESE ARE BEST DRUNK AT A PARTY,
SO THIS RECIPE MAKES ABOUT **8** DRINKS

This is the perfect holiday party drink. Keep a pot
of cider on the stove, leave out some coffee mugs,
and let your guests serve themselves, adding rum à
la carte. If you're hosting, alternate spiked cider with
virgin cider, at least until the guests leave.

Orange rounds

Coffee mug

VARIATION

TIP

Iced Apple Cider: Skip the cloves and cinnamon sticks, and the saucepan. Fill high-ball glasses halfway with ice cubes. Add 2 ounces rum, then top with cold cider and a pinch each of nutmeg and allspice. Garnish with orange round.

Don't boil this stuff, just keep it barely steaming. Tongue blisters are never appropriate.

cider

2   ounces **white rum**

2   ounces **dark rum**

2   ounces **vodka**

Splash of **grenadine**

4   ounces **orange juice**

2   ounces **passion-fruit juice** or ½ ounce **passion-fruit syrup**

INSTRUCTIONS

Put 3 cups crushed ice in a blender. Add all ingredients. Blend for 10 seconds, pulsing in additional 5-second increments if necessary. Pour into glasses, garnish with cherry and orange round, and serve.

GARNISHES

Maraschino cherries

Orange rounds

VARIATIONS

Tropical Storm: Leave out the vodka.

Tropical Depression: Leave out the vodka and the dark rum.

Pineapple Hurricane: Substitute pineapple juice for orange juice.

GLASS

Hurricane, duh

TIP

You could try this drink without the passion-fruit juice, but then it wouldn't be a Hurricane.

I've been a few places in this world, and I've had a few Hurricanes. Never have two been the same. But wherever bastardized versions are served, the Hurricane is unquestionably a New Orleans libation. This bastardized version, a frozen hurricane, is best served late on a stormy afternoon.

MAKES 2

DRINKS POTENT ENOUGH TO MAKE YOU IGNORE THE FORECAST (DRINK WITH SOMEONE YOU LOVE; IT COULD BE YOUR LAST)

frozen hurricane

planter's punch

8 ounces **white rum**

8 ounces **dark rum**

4 ounces **Cointreau**

Juice of 4 **limes**

8 ounces **pineapple juice**

8 ounces **orange juice**

1 ounce **grenadine**

1 teaspoon **bitters**

INSTRUCTIONS

Fill a pitcher halfway with ice cubes. Add all ingredients and stir well.

Place 4 or 5 ice cubes in each glass. Divide punch evenly among glasses. Garnish each glass with 1 grating *(no more)* of nutmeg and an orange round, and serve.

MAKES **1** PITCHERFUL, ABOUT **8** DRINKS

GARNISHES

Fresh **nutmeg**

Orange rounds

VARIATIONS

Frozen Punch: Halve the recipe and add all ingredients except garnish to blender. Fill halfway with crushed ice. Blend for 15 seconds, pulsing in additional 5-second increments if necessary.

Mexican Punch: Substitute tequila for the dark rum.

GLASS

Hurricane

TIP

Pour this out as soon as you mix it, or the ice will dilute your drink, making it taste funny and much less effective.

Planter's Punch is not to be drunk solo, not just because it's so strong, but because it inspires totally irresponsible, but still cute, party behavior. This is a party drink, through and through, best served in the afternoon, either on a deck or on the lawn.

There are lots of recipes for Mexican Coffee that call for tequila, but I think rum tastes better here. So I guess this isn't the world's most traditional Mexican Coffee recipe. Go ahead and contact my legal team.

mexican coffee

INGREDIENTS

1 ounce **Kahlúa**

1 ounce **dark rum**

Hot **coffee**

INSTRUCTIONS

Mix Kahlúa and rum in mug. Fill with hot coffee. Add a small dollop of whipped cream, then a few chocolate shavings. Serve hot.

GARNISHES

Whipped cream

Bitter chocolate shavings

GLASS

Coffee mug

VARIATION

Frozen Mexican Coffee: Use room-temperature coffee *(4 ounces per serving)* that's been brewed at double strength. Combine all ingredients, including whipped cream, in a blender with 1 cup crushed ice. Blend for 10 seconds, pulsing in additional 5-second increments if necessary, and serve in highball glasses. Shave chocolate over the top.

TIP

It's coffee, which means it's appropriate to drink for breakfast. Right?

MAKES **1** EYE-OPENER

Tequila Drinks

It's not just for *Gone Wild* nights. Tequila is an exquisite, sophisticated artisanal spirit made by men and women dedicated to and passionate about their craft and their product. It's one of the world's most refined spirits. So refine yourself: Skip the body shots and mix a real drink instead.

south of the border

INGREDIENTS

1½ ounces **tequila**

½ ounce **Kahlúa**

Juice of 1 **lime**

INSTRUCTIONS

Fill glass with ice water. Set aside.

Fill cocktail shaker with ice cubes. Add tequila, Kahlúa, and lime juice. Shake gently.

Break up brown sugar onto plate or wide-bottomed bowl. Don't leave any lumps. Use a fork to mix together with white sugar until evenly distributed. Dump out ice water from glass and rim with sugar mixture *(see page 35)*.

Give drink another shake, then strain into glass. Garnish with lime twist. *¡Olé!*

GARNISHES

Equal parts **brown** and **white sugar** for rimming glass

Long, thin **lime** twist

VARIATIONS

SOTB Caffè: Use a mixture of instant espresso powder and brown sugar to rim glass.

SOTB Caribe: Use coconut liqueur instead of Kahlúa.

GLASS

Cocktail, chilled

TIP

The better the tequila, the better your drink. Taste a few at your favorite Mexican restaurant, then invest in a good one.

At the end of the worst workday of your life, you may find yourself loading the car with a change of clothes and a map to Tijuana, where you'll drink yourself silly and embarrass yourself in front of a girl you thought actually liked you. Make a better choice: Hide the keys where you won't find them, and mix yourself a South of the Border or two.

Lots of people boycott bullfights because of cruelty to the bulls. Me, I think they should be boycotted because of cruelty to the matadors. Have you seen the pants they're forced to wear? Ouch. *(Don't let that visual discourage you from mixing this most excellent beverage.)*

matador

INGREDIENTS

2 ounces **white tequila**

1 ounce **Cointreau**

A few squeezes of **fresh lime juice**

3 ounces **pineapple juice**

INSTRUCTIONS

Fill cocktail shaker halfway with ice cubes. Add tequila, Cointreau, lime juice, and pineapple juice. Shake vigorously for 30 seconds and set aside.

Drop a few ice cubes in glass. Add garnish. Shake tequila mixture for 30 seconds more, then strain into glass and serve.

GARNISH

Lime round or pineapple wedge

GLASS

Highball

VARIATIONS

Apple Matador: Use apple juice instead of pineapple.

Frozen Matador: Combine ingredients in a blender with about 1 cup crushed ice. Blend for 10 seconds, pulsing in additional 5-second increments if necessary.

TIP

Use the purest pineapple juice you can find, not the reconstituted stuff with sugar added.

MAKES **1** LONG-SIPPING DRINK

2 ounces **white tequila**

4 ounces **freshly squeezed
   orange juice**
   (about 3 oranges' worth)

   Juice of ½ **lime**

½ teaspoon **grenadine**

Place 5 cubes in bottom of glass. Add tequila. Add orange juice. Add lime juice. Stir. Let sit 30 seconds. Tip glass to one side, and gently spoon grenadine down side of glass. *(It's significantly heavier than the other stuff, so it'll sink to the bottom. Then your drink, red on the bottom and orange-amber at the top, will look like a sunrise. Get it?)*

GARNISH

Lime rounds

GLASS

Highball

VARIATIONS

Frozen Sunrise: Combine all ingredients in a blender with 1½ cups crushed ice. Blend for 10 seconds, pulsing in additional 5-second increments if necessary. Serve in hurricane glass.

Tequila Sunset: Substitute blackberry brandy for the grenadine.

Tequila Noon: Skip the orange juice, lime juice, and grenadine and just do a couple shots of tequila.

TIP

Use white, not gold, tequila for this mellow drink.

tequila sunrise

MAKES 1 DRINK, BUT YOU'LL PROBABLY WANT ANOTHER

People either love or hate the Tequila Sunrise, but until you try one, you'll never know. The way this drink looks is just as important as how it tastes, so don't bother serving it in a paper cup. Well, OK, if that's all you've got, go for it.

frozen shady lady

MAKES **2** LADIES, ONE FOR YOU AND ONE FOR YOUR DATE

4   ounces **white tequila**

1   ounce **melon liqueur**

6   ounces **grapefruit juice**

INSTRUCTIONS

Combine tequila, melon liqueur, and grapefruit juice in a blender with 2 cups crushed ice. Blend for 15 seconds, pulsing in additional 5-second increments if necessary. Pour into glasses. Garnish with lime round and cherry, and serve.

VARIATIONS

Cherry Lady: Substitute cherry brandy for melon liqueur.

Lady Up: Fill bar glass or shaker base halfway with ice cubes. Add ingredients. Stir for 60 seconds. Strain into cocktail glasses.

Classic Shady Lady: Increase grapefruit juice to 8 ounces. Place a few ice cubes in glass. Add ingredients and stir. Garnish with lime round and cherry, and serve.

GARNISHES

Lime rounds

Maraschino cherries

GLASS

Highball

TIP

For a sweeter lady, use more melon liqueur. But start small with the stuff, because a little goes a very long way.

I don't usually go for drinks that are too fruity, but I'm all about the Shady Lady, which I first had at a hotel bar in Los Angeles. A few years later, I verified that this drink is best consumed in a hammock in Mexico, but the front porch will do in a pinch, especially for this frozen variation.

1 medium **seedless watermelon**, cubed

Juice of 1 **lime**

4 ounces **white tequila**

2 ounces **Cointreau**

½ teaspoon grated **fresh ginger** *(use your superfine hand grater)*

MAKES **2** **MIDSUMMER DRINKS**

(TRIPLE THE RECIPE FOR

A BLENDERFUL)

Process watermelon in a blender to a liquidy purée. Strain through fine-mesh sieve to remove most of the pulp *(don't worry about getting all of it, unless you want to)*. You should have at least 2 cups, but probably more like a quart, of juice. *(You can do this a day or so ahead of time; just keep it in the fridge.)* Save the extra for Watermelon Margaritas *(page 129)* later in the week.

Place 6 ounces watermelon juice, the lime juice, tequila, Cointreau, and ginger in a blender with about 3 cups of crushed ice. Blend for 15 seconds, pulsing in additional 5-second increments if necessary. Place lime round in bottom of each glass, then pour drink over the top. Garnish with mint sprigs and serve.

They say that necessity is the mother of invention, but the mother of *this* invention was boredom. And thirst. I first mixed this drink one night when the air conditioner in my way-too-hot fourth-floor New York walkup cashed out. I spent an hour sweating in bed thinking about drinks before getting up to make this, pour it into a roadie, and head out to the sidewalk for air. I met a lot of neighbors that night for the first time.

Lime rounds

Mint sprigs

Watermelon Mint Fizz: Place lime round and mint sprig in bottom of each glass. Muddle *(see page 50)*. Add a few ice cubes to each glass, then mix together 6 ounces watermelon juice with the remaining ingredients. Divide watermelon mixture among 4 glasses. Top with ginger ale and garnish with watermelon wedge.

GLASS

Highball

TIP

You can use a seed-filled watermelon, but get rid of the seeds, because they taste like crap when you send them through the blender. Bitter.

frozen watermelon mint cooler

2 ounces **tequila**

1 ounce **Cointreau**

Juice of 1 **lime**

½ teaspoon **simple syrup** *(page 29)* or ½ teaspoon **powdered sugar** *(optional, depending on how sour your limes are)*

Fill cocktail shaker with ice cubes. Add tequila, Cointreau, lime juice, and simple syrup and shake for 30 seconds. Set aside.

Rim glass with salt *(see page 35)*. Place lime round in bottom of glass. Shake margarita for 15 seconds more, then strain into glass. Serve immediately. *(If you'd rather have it on the rocks, place garnish in glass, fill halfway with ice cubes, and pour margarita over the top.)*

classic margarita

MAKES **1** SPECTACULAR DRINK

Most people think of a margarita as a summer drink, best enjoyed poolside in a pair of flip-flops with a whole mess of chips and salsa. And it is all of these things. But margaritas are also excellent even on the deadest days of the darkest winter, when the pasty skin on your forearms matches the skin on your ass.

GARNISHES

Coarse salt for rimming glass

Lime round

VARIATIONS

Cherry-rita: Substitute Heering
    cherry liqueur for Cointreau,
    and garnish with cherries
    and limes.

Watermelon Margarita:
    Substitute 1 ounce water-
    melon juice *(see page 126)*
    for the juice of one of
    the limes.

Frozen Margarita: Don't salt
    the glasses. Combine all
    ingredients in a blender with
    about 1½ cups crushed ice.
    Blend for 10 seconds, pulsing
    in additional 5-second
    increments if necessary, then
    serve in margarita glasses.

GLASS

Old-fashioned. Go figure.

TIP

Do yourself a favor and
get the good kind of tequila,
100 percent agave.

Fill bar glass or shaker base halfway with ice cubes. Add all ingredients except Dr Pepper and garnish. Stir gently for 60 seconds.

Place lime round in bottom of glass. Add 4 ice cubes. Strain booze mixture into glass, then top off with Dr Pepper. Stir and serve.

INGREDIENTS

½ ounce **white tequila**

½ ounce **gold tequila**

½ ounce **vodka**

½ ounce **white rum**

½ ounce **Cointreau**

½ ounce **sour mix** *(page 29)*

Dr Pepper

texas

This one's a lot like the aforementioned Long Island Iced Tea, in that it's a) got just about everything in it, and b) is hard to fuck up, and even if you do, you won't notice a thing after the first couple sips. Most recipes call for Coca-Cola, but this Dr Pepper version blows those away.

Lime round

Collins

VARIATIONS

TIP

Frozen Texas Tea: Using 4 ounces Dr Pepper, combine ingredients in a blender with 1½ cups crushed ice. Blend for 10 seconds, pulsing in additional 5-second increments if necessary.

Make sure your Dr Pepper is cold, so it daoesn't melt your ice too fast.

Tejano Tea: Substitute ½ ounce *reposado* tequila for the vodka.

Remember the Alamo: Add ½ ounce bourbon whiskey to the mix.

tea MAKES **1** INEBRIATING DRINK

Brandy Drinks

Save the good brandy—you know, that bottle of Armagnac you got for Christmas—for slow, late-night sipping after a long, wine-filled supper. Use the everyday stuff for pre-supper *(or pre-lunch)* mixed drinks.

2 ounces **brandy**

1 ounce **crème de menthe**

Fill cocktail shaker halfway with ice cubes. Add brandy and crème de menthe. Shake vigorously for 30 seconds. Strain into glass, garnish with mint leaf, and serve.

GARNISH

Mint leaf

GLASS

Cocktail, chilled

VARIATIONS

Vodka Stinger: Substitute vodka for brandy.

Mexican Stinger: Substitute white tequila for brandy.

TIP

If you want your stinger to last longer, serve it over crushed ice.

MAKES **1** OLD-SCHOOL COCKTAIL

Stingers, like old-fashioneds *(page 95)*, are fine to drink neat. **Just make sure you have dinner more or less prepared before you down this, or else it might end up *being* dinner.**

stinger

The sazerac is to the bartending world what the Aristocrats joke is to the stand-up comic world. **Bartenders order this delicate but broad-shouldered drink from other bartenders to measure their skills. Legend has it the sazerac originated in New Orleans, but it also might have come straight from God.**

sazerac

2 ½ ounces **brandy**

½ ounce **simple syrup**
(page 29)

A few dashes of **Peychaud's bitters**

A few drops of **Pernod**

Fill bar glass or shaker base halfway with ice cubes. Add brandy, simple syrup, and bitters. Stir gently and set aside.

Splash Pernod into bottom of glass. Place 3 or 4 ice cubes in glass. Strain brandy mixture into glass, stir only twice, then garnish with lemon twist and serve.

MAKES **1** OLD-SCHOOL DRINK

GARNISH

Lemon twist

GLASS

Old-fashioned

VARIATIONS

Bourbon Sazerac: Substitute bourbon for brandy.

Rye Sazerac: Substitute rye whisky for brandy.

TIP

Toast the Big Easy when sipping your Sazerac. It's good luck, and God knows they need some.

INGREDIENTS

1½ ounces **brandy**

½ ounce **crème de cacao**

½ ounce **half-and-half**

INSTRUCTIONS

Fill cocktail shaker halfway with ice cubes. Add brandy, crème de cacao, and half-and-half and shake gently for 30 seconds. Strain into glass. Garnish with 1 grating *(no more)* of nutmeg. Serve at bedtime.

MAKES **1** NIGHTCAP

One of the high points of the Golden Age of Cocktails *(1890–1930-ish, even though the freakin' feds tried to ruin everything with Prohibition)* was the invention of the Brandy Alexander, one of the best nightcaps ever conceived. Think of this as a liquid Ambien.

GARNISH

Fresh nutmeg

GLASS

Cocktail, chilled

VARIATIONS

Alex White: Substitute white crème de cacao.

Almond Alexander: Use only ½ ounce brandy and add 1 ounce amaretto to the mix.

TIP

Don't overshake this drink. It should be a little frothy, not foamy.

BONUS TIP

This drink is excellent poured over a couple scoops of vanilla ice cream.

brandy alexander

sidecar

INGREDIENTS

1 ounce **brandy**

1 ounce **Cointreau**

1 ounce **lemon juice**

½ teaspoon **simple syrup**
(page 29)

VARIATIONS

Blue Car: Substitute blue
curaçao for Cointreau.

Fizzy Car: Use Collins glass.
Pour cocktail over 3 or
4 ice cubes, then top with
club soda and stir.

INSTRUCTIONS

Fill cocktail shaker halfway with
ice cubes. Add brandy, Cointreau,
lemon juice, and simple syrup.
Shake vigorously for 30 seconds.
Set aside.

Place cherry in glass. Shake
brandy mixture for 15 seconds
more, then strain into glass
and serve.

GLASS

Cocktail, chilled

TIP

Taste your drink before serving.
Depending on how sour
your lemons are, it might need
more sugar.

GARNISH

Maraschino cherry

MAKES **1** DRINK

I had my first sidecar at Campbell's Apartment, **a cool
old-school bar upstairs at Grand Central Station. It
made perfect sense in the classic Gotham-era room.
I made my first sidecar a few weeks later at home.
Turns out it made perfect sense there, too.**

I guess the fact that this contains cranberry is enough to make it Nantucket-y. **God knows they've got enough cranberries up there. Best served after a long exhausting day lying around on the beach drinking beer.**

nantucket fizz

INGREDIENTS

2 ounces **brandy**

2 ounces **grapefruit juice**

Splash of **cranberry juice**

Club soda

INSTRUCTIONS

Fill bar glass or shaker base halfway with ice cubes. Add brandy and fruit juices. Stir gently for 30 seconds. Set aside.

Place 3 or 4 ice cubes in glass. Strain brandy mixture into glass. Top with club soda and stir. Garnish with lime round and serve.

GARNISH

Lime round

GLASS

Highball

VARIATIONS

Frozen 'tucket: Combine all ingredients except club soda in a blender with 1½ cups crushed ice. Blend for 10 seconds, pulsing in additional 5-second increments if necessary. Garnish and serve.

Vodka 'tucket: Substitute vodka for brandy.

TIP

A couple of these will make your sunburn feel better, but next time use some SPF, ya dumbass.

MAKES **1** FIZZ

2 ounces **Pisco**

1 ounce **sour mix** *(page 29)*

2 drops **Angostura bitters**

INSTRUCTIONS

Fill cocktail shaker halfway with ice cubes. Add Pisco, sour mix, and bitters. Shake vigorously for 60 seconds. Strain into glass, leaving a frothy head. Garnish and serve.

GARNISHES

Drop of bitters

VARIATIONS

Amaretto Sour: Substitute amaretto for Pisco.

Applejack Sour: Substitute applejack for Pisco.

GLASS

White wine

TIP

It's all about the froth in this drink. Shake with abandon.

MAKES **1** SOUR

Pisco is a regional riff on brandy for which the world owes Peru *(or possibly Chile, depending on who you ask)* a great debt of gratitude. **It's great to sip on rocks, but even better when shaken with sour mix and served straight up and ice cold.**

pisco sour

Beer and Wine Cocktails

Contrary to popular opinion, beer and wine are not always best left alone. Although perfect on their own, sometimes a little embellishment is called for. You know, like on birthdays, holidays, Mondays, Tuesdays. . . . Don't limit yourself to the cheap stuff in these mixes, either. My rule: If you wouldn't drink it straight, don't mix with it.

2 bottles inexpensive **Spanish red table wine**

½ cup **brandy**

1 **lime**, cut into rounds

1 **lemon**, cut into rounds

1 **orange**, cut into rounds

1 handful **red grapes**, cut in half

3 **underripe plums**, halved and pitted

2 **red apples**, sliced

Combine all ingredients in a large pitcher. Stir. Set in fridge to chill. Serve without ice.

There's a myth out there that says you should use crappy wine when making sangría. And I guess you could. But then your sangría would be crappy too. Here's what I say: Use an inexpensive wine, but not a crappy one. There are plenty out there. My favorite wine for sangría is Tempranillo, from Spain. You can usually find a good bottle for under $10. Ask for help at the wine store—they usually know what they're talking about.

This whole recipe is one big
garnish. Skip it.

VARIATIONS

White Sangría: Use white wine,
duh.

Champagne Sangría: Do we
need to spell this one out?

GLASS

White wine or **Mug**

TIP

Make this in the morning to serve
the same night, but don't keep
it for more than a day or two, or it
will get cloudy.

MAKES **1** PITCHER OF SANGRIA, THE MINIMUM YOU'LL NEED
FOR **4** OR MORE PEOPLE

bellini

1 tablespoon **peach purée** or **peach nectar**

Chilled **Champagne** or other **dry white sparkler**

INSTRUCTIONS

Spoon peach purée into glass. Top with Champagne, garnish with peach slice, and serve.

GARNISH

Peach slice

VARIATIONS

Nectar-ini: Use nectarine purée instead of peach.

Berry-ini: Soak a handful of raspberries in brandy. Drain and purée in a blender or food processor. Strain out seeds through a fine-mesh sieve, pressing on purée with back of spoon. Use instead of peach purée, and garnish with berry.

GLASS

Champagne flute

TIP

To make fresh peach purée, peel and pit 2 ripe peaches, then liquefy in a blender.

MAKES **1** ONCE-A-YEAR COCKTAIL

Some people swear by summer bellinis *(after all, the peaches are fresher then),* but as far as I'm concerned, bellinis taste best in the middle of the winter. Use the Champagne that's still sitting in your fridge from New Year's Eve.

For most of my life, I turned up my nose at mimosas, always opting for Bloody Marys or just straight-up Champagne with my brunch. But once I tasted one made with oranges that were squeezed before my eyes, I got it.

MAKES **1** WAKE-ME-UP

INGREDIENTS

3 ounces **freshly squeezed orange juice**

Chilled **Champagne** or other **dry white sparkler**

INSTRUCTIONS

Pour orange juice into glass. Fill with Champagne, add orange twist, and serve.

GARNISH

Orange twist

GLASS

Champagne flute

VARIATIONS

Apple-mosa: Substitute apple cider for orange juice.

Pome-mosa: Substitute pomegranate juice for orange juice.

TIP

Don't bother with reconstituted orange juice in these, just drink the bubbles. Use fresh juice.

mimosa

1½ ounces **gin**

Juice of ½ **lemon**

½ teaspoon **simple syrup**
(*page 29*)

Chilled **Champagne**
or other **dry white sparkler**

Fill cocktail shaker halfway with ice cubes. Add gin, lemon juice, and simple syrup. Shake vigorously for 15 seconds. Strain into glass. Top with Champagne, filling glass three-quarters full. Do not overfill. Garnish with cherry and serve.

french 75

As the story goes, this drink was named for the massive 75-millimeter guns the French used in World War I to launch artillery back at the Kaiser. In other words, it can get you blasted.

MAKES **1** BISTRO-WORTHY COCKTAIL

Maraschino cherry

Russian 75: Substitute vodka for gin.

Old-School 75: Add ½ ounce absinthe to the mix.

Collins

Mix this one short, and mix more as you go, so it stays cold while you sip.

The best beers for shandies are lagers, pilsners, and for those that like bitters, bitters. Don't use anything too flimsy, or the ginger ale will overpower it. But don't use anything too robust, like Guinness, or the ginger ale will get lost.

MAKES **1** MELLOW AFTERNOON DRINK

INGREDIENTS

6   ounces cold **beer**

6   ounces cold **ginger ale**

Generous squeeze of **fresh lemon juice**

INSTRUCTIONS

Pour beer and ginger ale into pint glass simultaneously. Add lemon juice and stir. Garnish with lemon wedge and serve.

GARNISH

Lemon wedge

VARIATIONS

Lime Shandy: Substitute lime
juice for the lemon juice, and
use Mexican or Thai beer.

Cider Shandy: Use hard cider
instead of beer.

PBR Shandy: Don't do it.

GLASS

Pint

TIP

Make sure all your ingredients are
ice-cold.

ginger shandy

red-eye

INGREDIENTS

8 ounces **beer**

1 ounce **vodka**

2 ounces **tomato juice**

GARNISH

Lime wedge

INSTRUCTIONS

Pour beer, vodka, and tomato juice into glass. Stir, garnish with lime wedge, and serve.

VARIATIONS

English Red-Eye: Use gin instead of vodka.

Mexican Red-Eye: Use tequila instead of vodka.

GLASS

Pint

TIP

Use the straight tomato juice, not the spicy stuff.

MAKES **1** MORNING-AFTER REFRESHER

The Bloody Mary gets all the ink as a morning-after remedy, but the red-eye is an excellent hangover cure. I think Mexican beers, particularly Negro Modelo or Bohemia, make the best red-eyes, but Beck's, a German lager, does a nice job too.

Ginger beer isn't available everywhere, so check out high-end stores like Whole Foods for brands like Reed's Ginger Brew. This is a smooth, easy drinking concoction, but beware—drinking too many too fast leads to a sucker-punch hangover. *(Trust me, I know.)*

dark and stormy

INGREDIENTS

4 ounces **ginger beer**

1½ ounces **dark rum**

Juice of 1 **lime**

INSTRUCTIONS

Pour ginger beer into glass. Top with rum and lime juice. Stir gently, then garnish with candied ginger and serve.

GARNISH

Candied ginger

GLASS

Collins

VARIATIONS

Lemon Storm: Add a few squeezes of lemon juice to the mix.

Florida Storm: Add 1 ounce fresh-squeezed orange juice to the mix.

TIP

You'll be tempted to use ice with this drink, but don't. It'll dilute your drink too much. Instead, chill your glasses in the freezer for ½ hour before mixing.

MAKES **1** STORMY DRINK

index

157

159

liquid measurements

Bar spoon = ½ ounce

1   teaspoon = ⅙ ounce

1   tablespoon = ½ ounce

2   tablespoons *(pony)* = 1 ounce

3   tablespoons *(jigger)* = 1½ ounces

¼   cup = 2 ounces

⅓   cup = 3 ounces

½   cup = 4 ounces

⅔   cup = 5 ounces

¾   cup = 6 ounces

1   cup = 8 ounces

1   pint = 16 ounces

1   quart = 32 ounces

750 ml bottle = 25.4 ounces

1 liter bottle = 33.8 ounces

1 medium lemon = 3 tablespoons juice

1 medium lime = 2 tablespoons juice

1 medium orange = ⅓ cup juice